COPYRIGHT 1987 by Bill Medcalf

All rights reserved. No part of this book may be used or reproduced in any manner without written permission from the publisher and author. All inquiries should be addressed to:

Bill Medcalf

127 Jellico Circle

Southlake, Texas 76092

ISBN 0-9620226-0-8

Printed by Taylor Publishing Company

Dallas, Texas

Helen Lance

Publications Consultant

Laser-Typeset by Esscorp Graphics

Dallas, Texas

RETRIEVE

A New, Gentle Approach

to Retriever Training

BILL MEDCALF

Illustrated By
Rae Galetka Mounts

Table of Contents

EQUIPMENT LIST 5
THE HUNTER 7
PICKING A PUP 11
DESIRE 13
HOUSE BREAKING 19
YARD BREAKING 29
    SIT: 29
    STAY: 30
    COME HERE: 31
    LIE DOWN: 31
    THE JUMPER: 32
    HEEL: 33
    DON'T BE GUNSHY: 34
BIRDS AND SINGLES 43
    BLINKERS, HARDMOUTH, and FLIERS: 44
    INSTRUCTIONS TO BIRDBOYS: 45
    THE BREAKING STRAP: 47
INTRODUCTION TO WATER 65
    HURRY UP METHOD 67
STRAIGHT LINE TO THE BIRD 71
    THE QUICK WHISTLE 72

BY LAND AND SEA	79
DECOYS	83
WORKING FROM A BOAT	87
DOUBLES ANYONE?	91
TAKING A "LINE"	99
LINING IN WATER	105
HANDLING	111
THE BASEBALL DIAMOND	111
THE CROSS PATTERN	122
THE DOUBLE CROSS	123
NEAR SIGHTED DOG	125
HARD OF HEARING	126
QUARTER AND FLUSH	137
TRACKING	141
TRAINING TIPS	144
HANDLING TIPS	147
THE HUNTING TESTS	153
SAMPLE TRAINING TESTS	157
GLOSSARY OF TERMS	180
QUICK REFERENCE FOR PROBLEMS	185
INDEX	189

EQUIPMENT LIST

Tennis ball

Choke Chain

Chest high waders

Coat hangers

Clothespins

Six Decoys

Small crate

Leash

Book matches

1 pair old socks

Pigeons or ducks

15 white retrieveing dummies

3 red retrieving dummies

6 feet of sash cord

1 foot long horseshoe

surveyors tape (1 roll)

RETRIEVE *Medcalf*

10 feet of single strand, insulated electrical wire

22 cal. blank gun

OPTIONAL EQUIPMENT

Lincoln Town Car

Pickup truck

50 feet of old fire hose

Retriever-R-Trainer

CHAPTER 1

THE HUNTER

I walked in a slow crouch, making the last fifty yards of my stalk in slow motion. The young retriever creeping at heel alongside me showed tension in every move. My pounding heart must have told him that something was going to happen....soon.

A few yards more, then I held my open hand in front of the dog's face. He stopped. Neither of us made a sound. I took two more steps and slowly stood up. Instantly the sky filled with beating wings, spray, and shouts of alarm from the large flock of ducks that flushed from the secluded little pond. The dog stood up when I shot, but stayed put. The "stop to flush" had been one of the most difficult parts of his training. I killed one of the greenheads clean, and scratched down another that flew over a hundred yards before he dropped and started swimming. The young dog was anxious to go. He marked the duck that fell close in, but the long cripple had fallen out of the dog's sight.

I called the dog to heel, quickly put my hand above his head and gave him the command "back." He made three bounds and leaped into the water. In less than a minute he came to heel with the dead Mallard. I lined him up, facing the spot where the cripple had fallen, and sent him again. When the dog got fifty yards out I could see that the cripple had moved to the right, trying to make it to some cattails growing close to shore. I gave one long blast on my whistle. The dog turned to look at me. I stuck my right arm out and yelled "over." He swam to my right. When he was on the direct line from me to the duck I blew the whistle again. He stopped and turned to me. With my arm straight over my head I yelled "back." He turned and swam straight to the cripple.

As he was making the long swim back with the Mallard Drake, I thought of the things a dog has to learn to be considered a "finished" retriever. He has to be obedient. He should be able to mark three or more shot birds and retrieve them, and take a "line" or direction from the handler to a bird that he did not see fall. He should respond to a whistle and take hand signals left or right, straight back, or to come in close. He will have to quarter and flush birds, then stop when they flush. He will track wounded game and retrieve it. Also he will be expected to sit, off lead and "honor," or watch another dog perform these things, without barking, whining, or worst of all, breaking. This book will teach you how to train your dog. I will take each step and show you how your dog can be a "hunting retriever," working on land, out of a blind, or from a duck boat that is surrounded by decoys. Training a dog takes just a few minutes each day for most things. Some of the field and water work will take more time, plus some help from friends to throw birds or dummies.

Keep the training periods short. Not over ten or fifteen minutes in the beginning. Punishment is having a loud "NO" yelled at him, not letting him get the bird, or being called in. I like to give a dog a lot of praise when he does what I want, and none at all when he does not. I do not recommend whipping, shocking, pinching ears, or any harsh training methods. Your dog will learn from positive reinforcement and praise. This book will show you how to train your dog...the gentle way.

CHAPTER 2

PICKING A PUP

It is often said that "gun-shy dogs are made, not born." That is not completely correct. I'm sure some dogs are "made" gun-shy, but some are more easily "made" than others. I believe dogs inherit shyness from their parents. If the parent dogs are afraid of loud noises, thunder, backfiring, gunshots, etc., their pups are likely to be the same way.

When looking for a dog to buy, there are several things that you should know about the parents. Is either of them afraid of noises?

Have their hips been X-rayed for dysplasia? Have their eyes been checked for hereditary eye diseases?

A dog or bitch that has bad hips should never be bred. Some people will breed them without ever checking. The buyer can put a lot of time and money into training a pup and discover that the dog is going to be crippled. The same applies to eye disease. It's tough enough for a dog with good vision to mark three or four shot birds and remember where they fell. If their eyes start to fail them at an early age, it will be impossible.

If you've checked the parents for gun-shyness, good hips, and hereditary eye disease, and all is well, start breaking the pup to guns at an early age. A section on "preventing gun-shyness" has been included in the chapter covering yard breaking.

CHAPTER 3

DESIRE

The first thing, and probably most important, is to build desire to retrieve. Start with an old boot sock rolled up tightly instead of a regular dummy. Dogs (young and old) can grab it easily, it does not hurt their mouth (if they are shedding teeth), and the sock will be used later to switch to bigger dummies, and birds.

Start soon after you get your pup home. Play with him using the boot sock rolled up so you can throw it. If it has not been washed, so much the better. Get in a hallway, or someplace that the pup can not run around you. Try to get the pup interested in the sock by flipping it back and forth and rolling it a few feet in front of him. After he becomes interested in chasing the sock and wants to grab it and play tug-a-war with you, throw the sock out and let him go for it. Don't try to restrain him now, just let him run after it. When he does get the sock try to coax him back to you. If he is not interested in chasing the sock, unroll it and flip it back and forth and tease him. When he shows interest, drag it along and let him catch up and grab it. When pup does anything that you want him to do---praise him for it.

I don't like for my pups, or older dogs, to carry, chase, pickup or chew on anything that is hard. Chewing hard objects makes a hard mouthed dog. A dog that is "hard mouthed" chews birds, crunches bones and may eventually eat them.

When you start throwing, or rolling the sock for your pup, sit spraddle legged on the floor and hold the pup in front of you. When you throw the sock let him go if he tries to chase it. Remember---we're trying to build desire, so don't start with sit and stay yet.

Throw the sock six or eight times and quit. A puppy's attention span is short and he will become bored if the lessons are too long. Let him make a few retrieves and quit while he still wants more. Don't give him the sock to play with after the session. Later on he will get excited when he sees the sock and knows that he is going to get to chase it and play "fetch." After he starts to get excited over this sock throwing, start "yard breaking." Chapter five consist of teaching him to sit, stay, come, heel, and lie down. Also included is "don't jump on me," and "don't be gun-shy." Before going into yard breaking, lets go back to the puppy.

While sitting spraddle legged as before, gently turn the pup facing away from you and push his hind end down while pushing slightly against his chest with the other hand. Hold him and throw the sock. After a couple of seconds, let the pup go. You might start telling him "fetch it up," "back," or whatever word you intend to use later as the command to retrieve.

Things don't always go as planned in dog training. When you come up with a problem, stop and think about it. The dog usually does not understand what you want him to do, so you have to think of a way to show him what you want. Here are some of the more common problems.

PROBLEM:

Dog does not want to chase after the sock.

SOLUTION:

1. Try building enthusiasm again by playing with the sock, a tennis ball, or toy. Wait a few days and try again. Try smearing a little bacon grease on the sock.

2. Make sure the pup isn't already tired from playing with kids or other dogs.

3. Get in a place where there are no distractions from what you are doing. No other socks, balls, or toys in sight.

4. Before you start the training session, give the pup time to relieve himself outside. Then start the training.

PROBLEM:

Dog runs to sock and picks it up, but will not bring it back.

SOLUTION:

1. That seems to be the normal thing with most dogs when starting to retrieve. Get in an area where the pup can't run around you. When he picks up the sock, clap your hands and try to coax him to you. If you are out in the field the dog will probably try to run back to the car or pickup with the sock, so you go to the area that he wants to run to and call him to you. Try throwing the sock or dummy and when the dog goes after it, move up closer to the fall. As the dog picks up the sock, start backing toward the car as you call him to you. As you back up, move over as necessary to stay in front of the pup.

2. If that doesn't work, put a light lead on the pup, throw the sock and send him for it. When he picks up the sock, gently pull him to you. You need to be easy with him so that he doesn't take it as punishment and drop the sock. Encourage the dog as you pull him to you. After a few times he will probably need only a tug to get him started. Any time you remove the lead and he refuses to return, put the leash on him again and leave it on for a few sessions. It won't be long until he learns that retrieve means "bring it back." Remember to praise the dog when he brings the sock...even if you had to gently persuade him.

PROBLEM:

Pup drops the sock when I tug on the leash.

RETRIEVE   DESIRE

SOLUTION:

1. With a very young dog, go to the sock and try throwing it again, with a lot of encouragement. Start the whole procedure over again.

2. For an older dog, take the dog out to the dummy or bird, tell him "fetch it up," grab the dogs upper jaw and put pressure on his upper lips (against his teeth) while forcing the dummy into his mouth. He will try to spit it out, or let it fall out, but be persistent. Keep cramming it back in his mouth, even if he lies down and rolls over. Tell him to "hold it." Always release the pressure on his lips the instant the dummy goes in his mouth. It helps to put your hand under his chin and hold his head up. Be sure to praise the dog when he does hold it for a few seconds. Let him know that's what you want him to do. Don't wear him out on this lesson. Keep it short and try to keep him happy about it.

Start your puppy retrieving dummies as soon as he gets big enough to drag them back. Slip one of the old socks over the end of a dummy, and the other sock over the other end. Now roll, or throw the dummy the same way you did the socks. The pup will go out to it and smell the old familiar socks and probably just grab the sock and drag the dummy back to you. After he has pulled it back a few times he will become a little more comfortable with the size and weight of the dummy. By the time the socks finally fall off, or are pulled off the dummy, the dummy will be familiar and he will bring it back without the socks. As enthusiasm builds, and the dog struggles to get loose to run after the dummy, start squatting down to call the pup to you, and stand up just as he reaches you.

Tell the dog "heel." Reach down with your hands and swing him around to the heel position. Make him sit by pushing down on his rump and push back on his chest while saying "sit." It will help get the dog to come all the way to you if you will back up slowly as he is coming in. When he gets four or five feet away, stop. He will probably run into you. Gently swing him around to heel, tell him "good dog" and then take the dummy from him.

Each stage of training takes time and patience. Don't hurry. Always quit the lesson with something that the dog can do easily; throw him a short single, or toss the sock, but don't throw "play" dummies or "happy bumpers." Some people swing a dummy, let the dog jump around barking, and then let him break to run after the dummy when it is thrown. I think they are undoing a lot of training by doing that, and teaching some bad habits, such as breaking, jumping up and grabbing birds out of your hand, and running off with the dummy. One time you let the dog break and run, the next time he is expected to stay until sent. Most dogs get confused easily enough without having to decide when you are serious and when you are not. He will be just as happy to get an easy retrieve that he can do blindfolded. Remember, a dog is learning something anytime he is out of his pen. He may have trouble distinguishing between "play" bumpers and serious ones and think that it's time to play when you think that it is time to work.

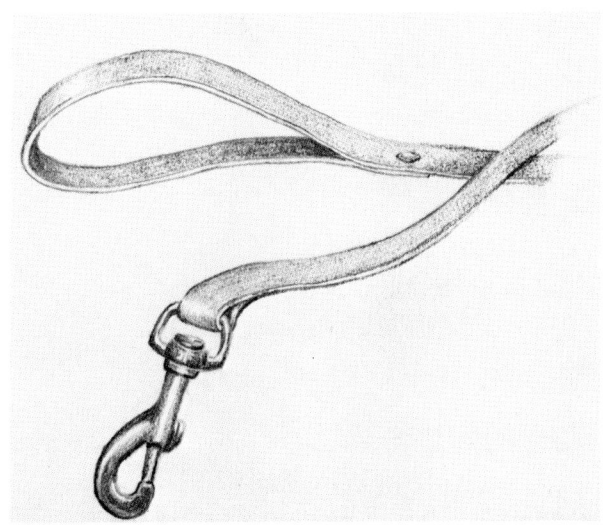

CHAPTER 4

HOUSE BREAKING

Some trainers don't recommend that you keep a hunting dog in the house. They say that making a pet out of a hunting dog will take away it's desire to hunt or retrieve. "Balony!" Thirty years ago, (in my bachelor days) I lived on a boat with a bird dog. Gracy had the run of the boat. She slept on my bunk, the couch, or anywhere she wanted to. She learned to go ashore when she needed to, and if we were not at dockside she managed to "hold everything" until we got back. This dog was definitely a pet. She was also one of the finest bird finders that I have had the good fortune to shoot over. We hunted extensively throughout the seasons. In addition to hunting quail, and pheasants, she was called on to retrieve all of the doves and ducks I shot. After the hunting seasons were all over we hit the field trial circuit. Gracy wasn't what is known as a "big going" dog, but she gave'em hell in the shooting dog stakes. She was even invited to compete in the National Shooting Dog Championship a couple of times. It is my opinion that Gracy, and many others since, worked harder for me because she was a pet.

If you want to make a pet out of your retriever, and keep the dog inside, house breaking is necessary. Start the house breaking as soon as you bring him home.

I could never understand the reasoning behind rubbing a dogs nose in it and flinging him outside when the dog had an "accident" in the house. Or, for that matter, whipping him with a newspaper. The dog probably doesn't understand either. Bowel movement is a natural function for a dog. If he poops on the floor and gets punished for it, he probably will think that he is being punished for doing what comes naturally, not for messing on the floor. Here is one way to house break a dog that is painless...for the dog, and for whoever does the clean up around the house.

Get a portable kennel large enough for the dog to be comfortable in, but small enough so that the dog cannot poop in one end, and curl up in the other to sleep. When you feed the dog, take all feed away from him around five or six every afternoon. This will allow the dog time to digest anything that he has eaten before you let him in the house at bed time. Before you go to bed at night take him outside and make him relieve himself.

Now you're probably asking yourself "how the heck do I make a dog relieve himself?" Well, there is an old trick that the field trial people use to clean out their dogs just before they run them in a series. It's called a "match stick enema."

Take the dog outside. Lift up his tail and insert a paper, or book match in the dog's rectum. The match goes in head first, about 1/2 inch deep. Just lock the dog between your legs with his south end pointing north, grab his tail with one hand and insert the match with the other. Hold the match in your mouth while you are getting the dog into position and your saliva will lubricate the match head. If the match falls out of the dog's rear end, get a new match and start over. You don't have to use a new match, but if you use the one that just fell out, you might consider some other form of lubrication. With the match in place, turn him loose and tell him to "take a break," or "go poop," or whatever command that you want to use. He will start looking for a place to go right away. When he squats, the paper match that you inserted will come out with everything else. After the dog has relieved himself, take him inside and put him in the kennel. Now he is in the best possible shape to last until morning, and not mess up his little cave. When you get up the next morning, have the back door open when you open the kennel, and usher him outside without delay. After a few days of this he will form a habit of going outside. He will also develop a habit of relieving himself before he goes to bed at night, and holding on until he is let out in the morning. Once the habit is formed, you can start letting him stay loose in the house. Just go through the same routine. The match stick enema usually isn't necessary after four or five days. He will develop a conditioned reflex to go when you tell him to "take a break." You can use this procedure to train him to use a certain area. When you take him out before bedtime, or first let him out in the morning, lead him to the spot you want him to go before you give him the enema. I teach my dogs to use my neighbor's yard. When the dog is in the house, in or out of the kennel, try to let him out every hour or so. It won't be long before he learns to let you know when he needs to go out. He will go to the door and bark or whine. Sometimes a puppy will come up to you and just start panting when he needs to go out.

If you want the dog to stay in a certain area, or lie on a special blanket, first put the blanket in the kennel and let him get used to it there. Then put that same blanket wherever you want the dog to sleep. A dog will soon learn that the blanket is safe ground when someone starts fussing at him. You will also soon learn to look there first, when you're missing a shoe, or a pair of gloves.

Another problem, especially with young dogs is chewing. They will chew furniture, shoes, pillows, carpets or just about anything that isn't distasteful to them. And believe me, very few things are distasteful to a dog. After thirty years of picking up scattered trash, discarding throw rugs, and hiding patent leather shoes that have been perforated with tiny holes the size of puppy teeth, I have discovered a simple way to stop dogs from chewing on things.

Last year I was camped out at a field trial in Canada. With me on the trip were Topaz and Ace, my two field trial candidates, plus six puppies that I let my wife talk me into bringing along. That was my first mistake. My next mistake was thinking that I could sell the pups before they got big enough to cause trouble. The pups rode in a big kennel that had a one half inch mesh wire floor built

HOUSE BREAKING

...above a drip pan in the bottom. This arran... ...ife's idea; and a good one. When the pups ..., everything dropped through the wire into ... stopped for fuel I would slip the pan out of ...nel and clean it. I stopped every one or two ...gs out to exercise. It wasn't long before the ...started waiting for me to let them out before ...emselves. Even very young dogs would rather ...dings. The puppies seemed to enjoy the short ...take care of their "high pressure warning ...k for something to play with or chew up.

...came when I camped out, which was nearly ... let the puppies out of the kennel, they picked up anything ... ey could carry, and ran off with it. They chewed on the tent ropes, my pants legs, and worst of all the nylon tent that I slept in. I had to do something before they destroyed all of my equipment. First I built a small, portable pen for the pups. I made the pen out of 2 x 4 inch mesh wire three feet high. There were four panels, four feet long, that I could fasten together with snap swivels to form a square pen. When I assembled the panels, I staked the edges down with tent pegs to keep the pups from rooting under the wire. This portable corral was a big help, but I still had to let them out occasionally so they didn't mess in it. I also had to keep them from attacking my tent when I let them out.

I had noticed earlier that the pups had not tried to chew on my pants legs when I sprayed insect repellent on my ankles. I wondered if the repellent would keep them from chewing on the tent.

I sprayed the edges of the nylon fly, and bottom of the ropes with "Off" before the next recess. When the pups were turned out, they made their usual race for the tent, gave it one sniff, and ran off playing together as if they didn't know that the tent existed. I had solved my biggest problem. From then on, I would just give anything that I wanted left alone a quick shot of repellent, and the dogs would totally ignore it.

PROBLEM:

What should I do when my dog has an "accident" on the floor.

SOLUTION:

1. First, put the dog outside. And don't be too nice to him while you are throwing him out. You may think that goes without saying, but...some say that if your dog is sick, or injured, you should make allowances. Well, the allowances that I would make for a sick dog would be to take him to a Vet Clinic, or put him in a pen outside. If you allow him to mess on the floor when he is sick, he will continue to mess in the same place after he gets well.

After you have cleaned up the mess, clean the place that he used with a mixture of water and vinegar to help get rid of the odor, then spray it with insect repellent to discourage him from going there again. Let the dog out at more frequent intervals, and watch for signals that he needs to go out. Barking, whining, restlessness, panting, and turning in a circle and squatting are some of the signals you might look for.

RETRIEVE   *HOUSE BREAKING*

My dog chews on furniture, shoes, and lamp cords when I let him in the house.

SOLUTION:

Get your pup a toy, or an old shoe to chew on. When he starts to chew on anything other than the toy or old shoe, scold him (verbally), and make him get on his blanket, or put him outside. If he still shows an interest in chewing on forbidden objects, give the object a shot of insect repellent to discourage him. Chewing on a lamp cord is usually self correcting.

This raised wire floor lets urine and droppings fall into the drip pan below. Helps keep the pups clean while traveling.

The pan slides out for easy cleaning.

RETRIEVE   *HOUSE BREAKING*

To make a dog "take a break" when you want him to...give him a "match stick enema."

To teach him "down," put your arm under his front legs....

...and pull his legs out, while pushing down on his back.

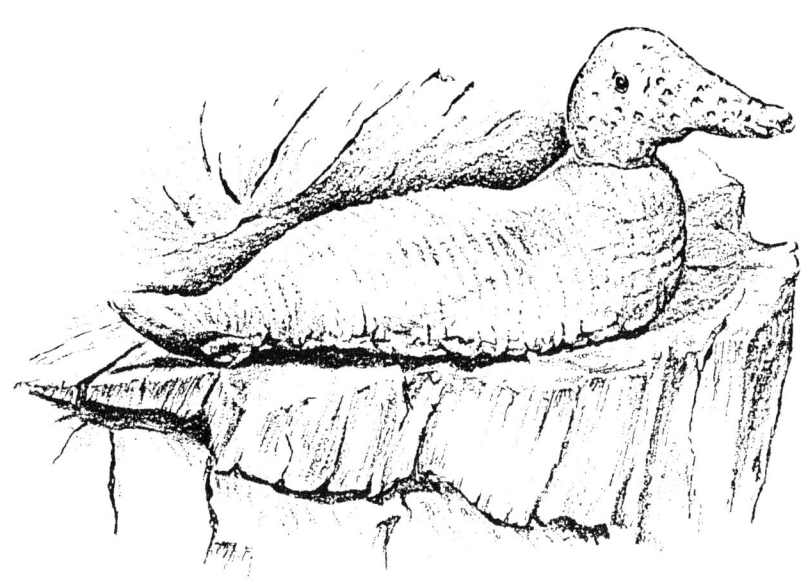

CHAPTER 5

YARD BREAKING

Yard breaking is a term commonly used for teaching a dog to sit, lie down, stay, come, and walk at heel. You should include "don't jump up on me." For retrievers add "getting used to a gun." With an older dog start a yard breaking session as soon as you bring him home. Keep the lessons short, not more than ten minutes or so.

SIT:

To teach your dog to sit, just push down on his rump and back on his chest while saying "sit." It sounds simple, and it is. The dog learns to associate the action with the command. If every time you say "sit" you push the dog into a sitting position, it will not be long until the dog anticipates the action and sits when he hears the command.

Start teaching very young dogs to sit when you throw the old sock, or dummy for them. While sitting spraddle legged, gently turn your pup facing away from you and push his hind end down while pushing slightly against his chest with the other hand. Hold him and throw the sock. After a couple of seconds, let the pup go. You might start telling him "fetch it up, back," or whatever word you intend to use later as the command to retrieve.

After the dog learns the voice command "sit," start giving one long blast on the whistle before you tell him "sit." Eventually he will start to sit when you blow the whistle. This will give you a head start later on, when you start to "handle" the dog.

STAY:

The command "stay" is next on the list. Some trainers don't teach a dog the command "stay." They say that "sit" does the same thing, that if a dog is "sitting" he is "staying." That may be true, but I like for my dogs to know that "stay" means just that. Stay where you are whether standing, sitting, lying down in the back of a pickup, or standing in a tub of bath water.

Get your dog to sit at your side, spread your hand out in front of his face and say "stay" in a strong voice. Take a few steps away from the dog, saying "stay" over and over. If the dog starts to come to you, and most of them will, just take him back to the spot where he was told to stay and gently push him into a sitting position again. Put your hand out as if you were stopping traffic and tell him "stay" while backing slowly away. Every time the dog starts to come to you before you call him, put him back and start over.

COME HERE:

After the dog learns to stay where you put him, teach him the command "come," or "here." Put a leash on the dog and tell him to stay. Walk to the end of the leash and say "here," and give a slight tug or jerk on the leash. The dog will usually be glad to run to you. When he does, don't forget to praise him. Make him sit, and then go back to the end of the leash again and call him to you. You can use a "sit, stay, here, heel" drill a few times every day and have the dog working like a champ in no time at all.

LIE DOWN:

The command "down" is another command that your dog should learn. I like to have a dog lie down when I'm hunting geese over a spread of decoys. It gives us a lower profile, and helps keep the dog out of sight. It's also nice when the dog is in the house standing between you and the T.V. and you can't see over him.

To get a dog to lie down, first get him to sit. Then put your arm under his front legs and just ease his legs out in front of him. You probably will have to hold his rear end down, but after a few sessions he will catch on to what you want when you say "down." After he starts to respond, just point at the ground and say "down." Then push his rump down and pull his front legs out. After a few days most dogs will start to respond to the pointing. If you go into the obedience show ring with your dog you will notice that the obedience trainers hold their hand straight up for the signal to lie down. I use this (hand held over head) to send a dog away from me when giving him hand signals. Hand signals will be covered in the chapter on handling. But to keep from confusing the dog later on, teach your dogs "down" by pointing at the ground.

THE JUMPER:

Dogs can be very affectionate pests. The biggest pest of all is the one that thinks he has to have his feet on your shoulders for you to pet him.

When a little puppy jumps on you, grab his muzzle like "crow picks on a baseball bat" and push him down. Just wrap your hand over his nose and mouth and force him down and away from you. With a larger dog, push down on his muzzle and give him a swift knee in his chest. This will usually discourage him from jumping on you. To teach the dog not to jump on other people, encourage the dog to jump up on you by calling and patting your chest. When your dog jumps up...step on his toes, or give him a knee in the chest. Continue to do this until the dog learns that jumping up isn't the best way to get affection. Don't wear golf shoes, or hobnail boots during this phase of training. You need to consider the possibility of injuring the dog's toe or foot, so use soft sole shoes, and some discretion.

Most dogs can learn these commands in a few days, but like anything else, if you don't use it you lose it. After the dog learns the yard training, put him through a one minute drill every now and then just so he doesn't forget.

HEEL:

Heel is another important command for the dog to learn. He has to heel properly before he can learn to take a "line" to a bird or dummy. Most dogs are taught to heel on the left side. In a field trial, or hunting retriever test, it doesn't make any difference, but if you intend to show your dog in obedience or in bench competition, he will be required to heel on your left.

To teach a dog to heel, call him to you and tell him "heel." When he comes, grab his collar with one hand and with the other hand swing him around by your side into the heel position. I like to use a "choke chain" for a training collar. The choke chain grabs, or tightens around the dog's neck when you jerk on it and slacks off when released. It is painless, and shouldn't be confused with the German Pinch collar. The pinch collar is designed to pinch the dogs neck in several places and create pain. The choke chain does not hurt, but it does get the dogs attention.

With the collar and leash, put the dog at the heel position on the left side. Start off at a walk and tell the dog "heel." When you say "heel" give a little jerk on the leash. If the dog lags behind give him another jerk. If he runs out in front give him a jerk and bring him alongside. Every time you correct the dog with a jerk on the leash give him a verbal correction. Don't be too hard on him. Most young dogs are frightened when they are started on a collar and leash. Be patient when the pup runs between your legs or tries to pull away from you. He'll catch on eventually. After you get your dog to a point where he doesn't fight the lead, start walking in a straight line. After ten or twelve steps make a turn left or right. Every time you turn give the leash a light jerk and say "heel." When you stop, make the dog sit at your side. That may require you to push down on his rear end, or take your hand and position him as you want him. Remember to praise the dog when he does something right is as important as punishment when he does it wrong. When teaching the dog to come to heel, step back with the left leg as the dog is coming to you. When the dog starts to turn to face forward move your leg up even with the right. This movement seems to help a dog get lined up properly. (see illustration pg. 58)

Show dog people have their dogs circle behind them on the right side and come to heel on the left. That is good for show dogs, but when my dog retrieves a bird or dummy I don't want him circling behind my back. I want him at heel holding that bird and thinking about where the next bird is. While he is showing everyone how pretty a Cock Pheasant is, a cripple may be running off. It's bad conservation to let cripples get away. The longer a dogs' attention is away from the marks, or shot birds, the harder it is for him to remember where they fell.

DON'T BE GUNSHY:

Yard breaking does not normally include "getting used to gunfire," but it is so important for a retriever that I include a short section on it.

At feeding time, walk off fifty yards or so while the dog is preoccupied with eating and shoot a 22 caliber blank gun. Do this every time you feed the dog. After he seems to get used to the noise, move a little closer when you shoot. It won't take long before the dog will associate the noise and smell of gunpowder with some-

RETRIEVE   YARD BREAKING

thing good...eating. That is normally all it takes to keep a dog from developing a fear of guns. I also caution you about kids and firecrackers. Do not ever, under any circumstances let anyone pop firecrackers around your dogs. That applies to old or young dogs. A hunting dog should associate gunfire, or anything similar, such as blanks or firecrackers, with hunting. After some fun loving kid throws a couple of cherry bombs at your dog, or gets after him with one of those whistling chasers, your dog will probably tuck his tail and slink off every time he hears a door slam.

PROBLEM:

The choke chain doesn't slack off when I release pressure on the leash.

SOLUTION:

There are two ways to put the choke chain on the dog. If the dog is to heel on your left, the proper way is to slip the collar on the dog so that the part of the chain that you will attach the leash to will come over the top of the dog's neck and slip through the ring that comes up form the bottom. Here is an easy way to remember. If the dog is to heel on your left side, face the dog and form the letter "P" in front of the dog with the choke chain and then slip it over his head. If the dog will heel on your right side, form the figure "9" with the chain and slip it over the dog's head. That way the bottom ring will naturally fall down and loosen the chain when pressure on the leash is released. If the collar is slipped over the dog's head incorrectly, the chain will remain tight when pulled. Check the illustrations and learn the proper way to put the collar on the dog.

PROBLEM:

When my dog sits, he sits facing me or some way other than at my side.

SOLUTION:

1. Most dogs want to sit in front of you instead of at your side. As your dog is coming to you, step back with your left leg. As the dog turns to sit in front of you, move your leg forward and turn your body 90 degrees to your right. This move will put the dog (that has just sat) at your side, and in the proper position.

2. Another thing you can do is tell the dog to sit. Put pressure on his rump and push back on his chest. With the hand that is pushing the rump, pull or push the dog into the position in which you want him. Don't ever praise or pet the dog until he is in the proper position. Always insist that he sit properly. It will be important later on when teaching him to take a line.

PROBLEM:

I tell my dog to stay. When I walk away he slinks on his belly and tries to follow me.

SOLUTION:

1. Any time the dog does not stay where you tell him, walk back and pick him up or drag him back to the designated spot. Set him down and loudly reinforce "STAY!"

2. If you have a dog that absolutely will not stay, chances are that he is afraid that you are going to leave him and not come back. Most dogs want to follow you because they are afraid of missing out on the action. In either case, you have to instill confidence in the dog that you will return.

There is a simple device that I use to keep a dog in place while I walk out in the field. I call it "the foot long horseshoe." It consists of a piece of 1/2 inch steel bar that is bent into a horseshoe shape about ten or twelve inches long, and four inches wide. The horseshoe is driven into the ground with the bend at the top sticking up about two or three inches. I use that for a stake. Get a piece of nylon line 100 feet long and tie a snap swivel on one end of it. Slip the end of the line with the snap on it, through the top of the stake that is sticking up above the ground, and snap it on the dog's choke collar. Hold the nylon line and walk out in the field. The dog can't follow as long as you keep the line tight. You can throw a dummy, shoot a bird, or call the dog to you, and the dog can only leave the spot at the stake when you release the line that you are holding. When you let go of the line, it will slip through the stake as the dog runs to you. Hold your dog with this device while you walk out and throw dummies, work on a fence, or whatever. He will soon learn that you will come back and let him in on the action. This same rig will help when you move out of sight of the dog that has been told to "stay."

PROBLEM:

My dog runs away when I tell him to come.

SOLUTION:

1. Chances are, the dog has been called in at one time or another and then whipped. Never whip a dog after you have called him to you. When a dog runs away or just sits out in the field and looks at you, there is a strong probability that he doesn't know what you want him to do. Go get the dog and bring him back. Try to show him what you want. Walk him through the test. If necessary, go back to the beginning. If you lose your temper, don't do anything. Just put the dog back in his kennel and try again another day.

A friend of mine asked if I could teach her Yellow Lab to "come when called." She said the dog ran off every day, and she would jump in her Lincoln and go find him and bring him back. The only punishment Buckwheat received was a "bad boy!" when she put him in the car. She did make him ride in the back seat instead of the front. He quickly learned to make a game of running off, and got so spoiled that he wouldn't ride in anything but a Lincoln Town Car.

The next day I took several dogs to a big pond to do some water training, and Buck came along to get his first lesson on "come here."

I parked my truck, and let all of my dogs out to stretch their legs before the training started. When I opened the kennel door, Buckwheat bolted past me before I could get a leash on him, and headed for the water. He played with the other dogs and was having a big time until I whistled for them to come in. All of the dogs came to me, except Buck. He stopped about fifty yards out, and wouldn't come closer.

I walked toward him and squatted down, trying to coax him to me. When I called and clapped my hands, he would yap at me and run farther away. With me slogging along in hip boots, we traipsed to the north fence line and then turned West, toward the interstate.

I was concerned about the dog getting on the freeway, so I started jogging, trying to catch up. Five minutes later the dog crossed a fence and was on the highway. I hurried over the fence, ripping the top out of one of my boots and the crotch out of my pants. Southbound we went, down the interstate. The dog frolicked back and forth across the busy road, stopping only to investigate some vile smell, or to leave his mark on the mileage posts. I was doing the scout's pace , with hip boot flapping and sweat flying, determined to keep the dog in sight.

The chase continued. As we passed the second mile marker, I slowed to a limp, and became aware of the blisters on my feet. At the third mile I noticed the raw burning on my ankles. I couldn't give up. The dog looked like he was tiring, and I was planning ways to stake him out on the highway when I caught him. He finally slowed to a walk and started looking back, as if wondering when the Lincoln would show up. I was also looking back, to see if my friend was coming with the pickup. Another mile post went by. I thought I could feel my boots filling with blood.

We were on an overpass when Buck crossed in front of an eighteen wheeler. My shouts at the dog were drowned out by a continuous blast of the diesel's horn. The despairing blend of squalling tires and screams from the dog changed my feelings from acrimony to anguish. Sucked into a vacuum as the truck roared past, the dog tumbled over and skidded into the guard rail. Before I could get to him, he regained his feet and started running again. I couldn't go much farther. As I was about to give up, another diesel roared down the hill. I played my last trump. I yelled at the dog, and when he looked at me, I turned and walked the other way.

As the truck passed, I glanced back. Buckwheat looked as if he wanted to follow me. Slowly, I kept walking away, and patted my leg to encourage him. He trotted up behind me with tail wagging, and started licking the sweat off my hands. My persistence had finally paid off. I snapped a leash on him and started walking north.

When Durke pulled up with the truck I opened the tail gate and told Buck to get in. He didn't hesitate for one second. Maybe he thought the Lincoln had broken down and that truck would be his last chance for a ride home. I like to think that he realized he was going to do what he was told, even if it killed both of us.

I painfully climbed into the front seat, and pulled off my boots. Durke couldn't get over the fact that the dog was still alive.

"Yes," I said. "It's a miracle that a car didn't hit him."

"Car hell!, I thought you would strangle him when you got your hands on him."

Later that day, I was putting the dog in his kennel when the owner stopped by.

"Well, how'd the training go today?"

"Not too bad." I said. "He has already learned to like riding in a pickup truck."

I never had trouble getting that dog to come to me after that.

If the dog is to heel on your left side, face the dog and form the letter "P" in front of the dog with the choke chain and then slip it over his head.

If the dog will heel on your right side, form the figure "9" with the chain and slip it over the dog's head. That way the bottom ring will naturally fall down and lossen the chain when pressure on the leash is released.

RETRIEVE

"STOP THAT NOISE!" To make a dog stop barking or whining, squeeze his mouth together and tell him to be quiet.

For field trials or hunting, teach your dog to "down" (lie down) by pointing to the ground.

CHAPTER 6

BIRDS AND SINGLES

By now your dog should have a strong desire to retrieve a sock or dummy, and be well started on yard breaking. The main objective of this book is to teach your dog to retrieve birds, so lets get the pup started on birds.

I use pigeons for the introduction to birds. They are hardy, can be purchased in most areas, and don't cost much. Some places, such as Canada, do not allow the use of live birds in training or field trials. Check your local laws. Get one of the old socks that you have been using and cut a hole in the toe big enough for the birds head to go through. Stuff a pigeon into the sock with his head sticking out. Get in an area that has thick grass and roll or toss the pigeon out a short distance. The grass will help cushion the fall when you toss the bird. Send the dog as before. When he runs out to the bird he will probably grab one end of the sock and drag it back. The bird may seem strange to him but the familiar smell of the old sock will give him confidence. After the pup has retrieved the bird in the sock several times, the bird smell and feel will become familiar and he won't care if the bird is in the sock or not.

BLINKERS, HARDMOUTH, and FLIERS:

You can use this same technique to introduce the dog to ducks, pheasants, and other birds. If you use live birds the only thing I would do differently with the larger birds is tape their bills closed so that they can't peck the dog. After your dog has retrieved live birds for a long time he won't pay much attention to the bird pecking on him. A young dog may develop a fear of some birds and resort to what is known as "blinking." A blinker is a dog that knows the bird is there but avoids it. A blinking retriever will hunt all around a bird and act as if he can't find it. Some will smell the bird, associate it with bad memories and head the other way.

To prevent the cruelty of a "hardmouth" dog killing or injuring birds, all birds that are used in A.K.C. sanctioned or licensed field trials are either thrown as dead birds or shot as "fliers." A flier is a live bird that is thrown into the air and shot while it is flying.

I still use live pigeons and ducks to train dogs. Rubber bands wrapped around the legs and wings of birds keep them from getting away when they are thrown for the dogs. If I know that a dog is "hardmouth," or has a tendency to be rough on the birds, I use only dead birds for that dog.

"Hardmouth" is when a dog chews on, or crushes the bird, making it unfit for the table. Hardmouth is easy to prevent, but difficult to cure. To keep a dog from developing hardmouth, do not let him chew on sticks or hard objects. When he picks up a bird insist that he bring it to you without delay. If you see him chewing a bird get to him as quickly as you can and take the bird away. Try to discourage the dog from biting down on the bird by putting your hand partially in the dog's mouth while he is holding the bird. When throwing live or dead birds in water use pigeons or ducks. Pheasants get water-logged quickly and are more conducive to making a dog chew or bite down on the birds. Another thing that will help is to take the intestines out of dead birds. The birds will stay fresh much longer, and can be used for several days if kept refrigerated when not in use. When a bird starts to come apart, or is badly shot up, throw it away and get a fresh one.

INSTRUCTIONS TO BIRDBOYS:

Birdboy is the common term for any boy, girl, or adult that throws birds for a dog to retrieve. All retriever field trials use birdboys to throw birds and plant "blinds." If you are called on to be birdboy, there are a few important things that you should know. Do not talk, move around, or swing dummies around while you are out in the field. A handler may be trying to get his dog to look at another gunner, or birdboy. That is difficult if you are attracting the dog's attention by moving around or making noise.

RETRIEVE   *Medcalf*

Keep all dummies and birds off of the ground. If a dog picks up a dummy laying at your feet instead of the one he was sent for, he will learn to go to the birdboy instead of marking the bird that was thrown. If a dog comes to you, hold the birds up so he can't get to them. He will soon learn to hunt for the one that was thrown.

When you are throwing birds for several dogs, be consistent. Try to make the bird land in the same place each time. Sometimes it helps to mark the spot with a rock or stick.

Try to throw the bird, or dummy about twenty or thirty yards. That is the distance that most birds will be shot.

"Keep em up!" is a common cry from the trainer. What he means is, throw the birds or dummies high. The longer a dog sees a dummy in flight, the longer he will remember it. If a dog is expected to mark several birds, such as a double or triple, help him remember where they fall by throwing the birds with a long arc.

Throwing dummies "ain't as easy as it seems." You want a high arc, long distance, and for all dummies to land in a three foot circle. More dog trainers get divorced as a result of their wife throwing birds for them than any other thing. So if your bird thrower sails one 100 feet in the air and it lands behind him, don't be too quick to chew him out. Just have him pick it up and try again. When a bird is thrown badly in a field trial, the judges will call a "no bird" and have the birdboy pick up the bird. They ask you to take your dog off the line, and after a couple of dogs have run, they will let your dog have another go at it.

Do not try to help a dog unless the handler tells you to. One year in San Antonio I was practicing for a field trial. A teen-age boy, that was watching my Chesapeakes, asked me if it was true that Chessies would only work for their trainer. I told him that my granddaughter handles the dogs, and asked him if he would like to try. I gave him some instructions on how I like my dogs to be handled, and let him throw a few bumpers for "Ace." Well, Ace and Mark really hit it off. At the trials the next day, the judges set up a "water triple," and Ace's new friend was one of the birdboys. Ace picked up the first two birds, and then started for the last one. He swam straight for the bird for the first seventy-five yards, and when he was thirty yards away, Mark yelled "go get it Ace." Well, Ace got it, but I figured that would be all for this trial. You are not allowed to shout encouragements to a dog that is working.

After Ace retrieved the bird, one of the judges put his clipboard down and walked over to me. "I didn't hear that birdboy yell 'go get it' to your dog. Did you?"

Retrievers not only have to learn to look for birds that have been shot, but also to use their nose to help find them. Have your bird boys throw some birds in heavy cover. The dog should see the bird thrown, but not be able to see the bird after it is on the ground. This will help the dog remember where it landed and use his nose to help locate it. If you don't have any suitable cover handy where you are training, use red dummies. Dogs don't see red well, and will have to use their nose to find them.

THE BREAKING STRAP:

A retriever should not "break" to run after a bird. He should stay at heel until sent by the handler. To teach the dog not to "break," I use a homemade training aid I call a "breaking strap."

This is a piece of 3/8 inch nylon rope, or sash cord that is used to restrain the dog while you or someone else throws a dummy. Get a piece of rope about six feet long. Tie a small loop in the middle. In one end tie a loop that will just fit over your hand. The other end is left without a knot so that it will slip through the small loop. If you heel your dog on your left side, put the end loop over your left wrist. Put the free end of the rope around the dog's neck and through the small loop. Now you can hold the free end of the rope with either hand, and when you are ready to send the dog just say "back" and release the end you are holding. The rope will slip free as the dog runs after the bird. With this release rope you can hold him easily with one hand, throw the dummy with the other, and then give him a line using your hand for direction. Some trainers slip the free end of the rope through the ring on the collar instead of around the dog's neck.

I use the breaking strap until the dog is steady. By steady I mean that he will stay at sit or heel while I throw the dummy, then go for it only after sending him with the command "back." When he is steady with the strap on, try him without it. If the dog breaks, don't let him get the bird or dummy. Instruct your bird thrower to pick it up before the dog can get it. Try to yell the dog back by "**NO, HERE**, or **HEEL**." Go out in the field if necessary and bring the dog back to the line. Let him know that you are not happy with him.

If you are throwing the dummies or birds yourself and the dog breaks and gets the dummy, just go to him (while he is returning) and take the dummy from him. Don't be gentle when you take it. No "good dog" or praise. He will know that he has done something wrong. A smart dog thinks that he won't be punished as long as he has the bird or dummy, so it is important that you don't do anything that will be taken as praise when he breaks to pick up a bird. Try to yell the dog back when he breaks, but if he still goes out and picks up the bird, walk rapidly out to the dog and snatch the bird away. Don't say anything. Roughly snap a leash on him, walk him back and start over. If the dog breaks again and won't stop, or come back, go back to the breaking strap. When the dog does wait until sent, don't forget to praise him for it.

Don't make your dog wait too long before sending him for the bird. I like to put my hand above his head before sending him. It will help later on when he has to "honor" while another dog retrieves. If your dog is hesitant about retrieving, and doesn't show a lot of enthusiasm, don't try to steady him now. He may become so steady that he won't go pick up the bird. Work on building enthusiasm and save the steadying for later. Now let's put a little diversion into the retrieve.

Any change in terrain, from plowed ground to grass, a road, a small ditch or a creek will be enough to stop a young dog. A dog that has not done much retrieving will usually run out to where the cover changes and start looking. Dogs like to go back over terrain, or through water on the same trail they have just been over. With this in mind, take your dog, young or old, on a leash and walk him out to where the dummy will fall and walk him back. Now he has been over the line that he will take to the bird, through the creek, across the road or whatever.

Have someone throw a dummy. When you send the dog he probably will go on out to it because he has already been across all of the terrain and feels confident that no harm will come when he goes out there again. If you want to stretch the dog out, and have him make longer retrieves, start by sending him on a short retrieve. As he returns with the dummy, you back up twenty five or so yards. Throw another in the same place (or have someone throw for you) and send him again. While he is returning with that one back up another twenty five yards.

You can have a young dog making very long retrieves in this way. A dog will build up a mental "wall" if he makes all retrieves within a certain distance. If you are throwing dummies out no farther than seventy five yards, the dog will soon take that as his maximum range, and not go any farther no matter how far away the dummy is. If you have this problem with a dog, start walking back on him when he retrieves and he will soon be making retrieves from very long distances.

In the early stages of training, set up the tests so a cross wind is blowing from where the bird will land, toward the thrower (see sample training test). Most inexperienced dogs will start toward the bird that has been thrown, and then run to the birdboys. If that happens, scent blowing from the bird will draw him back to the bird and help him make a successful retrieve.

RETRIEVE   BIRDS AND SINGLES

(see illustration pg. 159) Later I will tell you how to teach a dog to hunt in the area of a fall no matter what direction the wind is from.

PROBLEM:

When switching from socks to dummies, or from dummies to birds the dog doesn't pick up the dummy or bird.

SOLUTION:

At the start of a session, throw the sock a few times and then slip one or both over the dummy and tease the dog with it before throwing. With an older dog, go back to "fetch it up," run out and put the dummy in his mouth and encourage him to bring it back to where you threw from. If necessary, put the dummy in his mouth and hold it there with one hand while you drag him back by his collar with the other. When you and the dog (holding the dummy) get back to the line, don't forget to praise him. That is the way he learns what you want.

PROBLEM:

The dog hunts short of the area of the fall.

SOLUTION:

1. Most trainers I know have the bird throwers pick up the dummy, yell to attract the dogs attention, and then toss the dummy again. I don't think that is the best way to help the dog learn what you want. I have seen dogs that run out in the field, stop, and wait for someone to toss the bird up for them. I prefer to go to the area of the fall and encourage the dog to find the dummy. When your dog hunts short or gives up the hunt and starts to come back to you, hustle out to the area of the bird, clap your hands and tell him to "hunt it up." Later, when he has trouble finding a bird in heavy cover he will not be inclined to quit hunting and look for help. He'll know he is going to have to continue hunting until he finds the bird.

2. Move the dog closer to where the dummy will fall and throw one. Move back as the dog returns. Keep doing that until you get back as far as you want the dog to retrieve from.

Another thing you can do is lead the dog, on a short leash, out to the area of the fall. Walk the same line that you want the dog to take. You and the dog go to the fall area, then about halfway back to the line. Have the birdboy throw one and send the dog. If he still does not go to the area, move closer and do it again. When he retrieves the dummy move farther back and send him for another thrown in the same place. Continue working him back until you get him working at the distance you want.

A drill that you can use to teach your dogs to hunt in the area of the fall is to have the birdboy alternate the throws so that he throws one at an angle back, then the next one straight out, then another back, then one closer in. (see diagram pg. 54) Keep alternating the throws and the dog will learn to hunt the area around the birdboys, or the gunners in field trials.

Here is another important thing to remember. When throwing birds for the young or inexperienced dog, don't throw a mark so that a dog has to go through the area of an old fall to get it. An example would be to throw a bird out about seventy five yards and send your dog for it. Then have your bird thrower move straight back fifty yards and throw another on the same line. The dog will take the initial line out toward the second bird, but when he runs into the leftover scent from the first bird he will start to hunt there. It will confuse the dog if you take him out of that scented area now and make him hunt farther back. Try to avoid situations that are confusing. Keep plenty of angle between the marks you throw for an inexperienced dog.

RETRIEVE

Medcalf

To teach your dog to hunt in this area...

1st -- Have the birdboy throw one back.

Then have him throw the next one straight out.

Throw the next closer in.

Then throw one out again.

By alternating throws your dog will learn to hunt the area around the birdboy

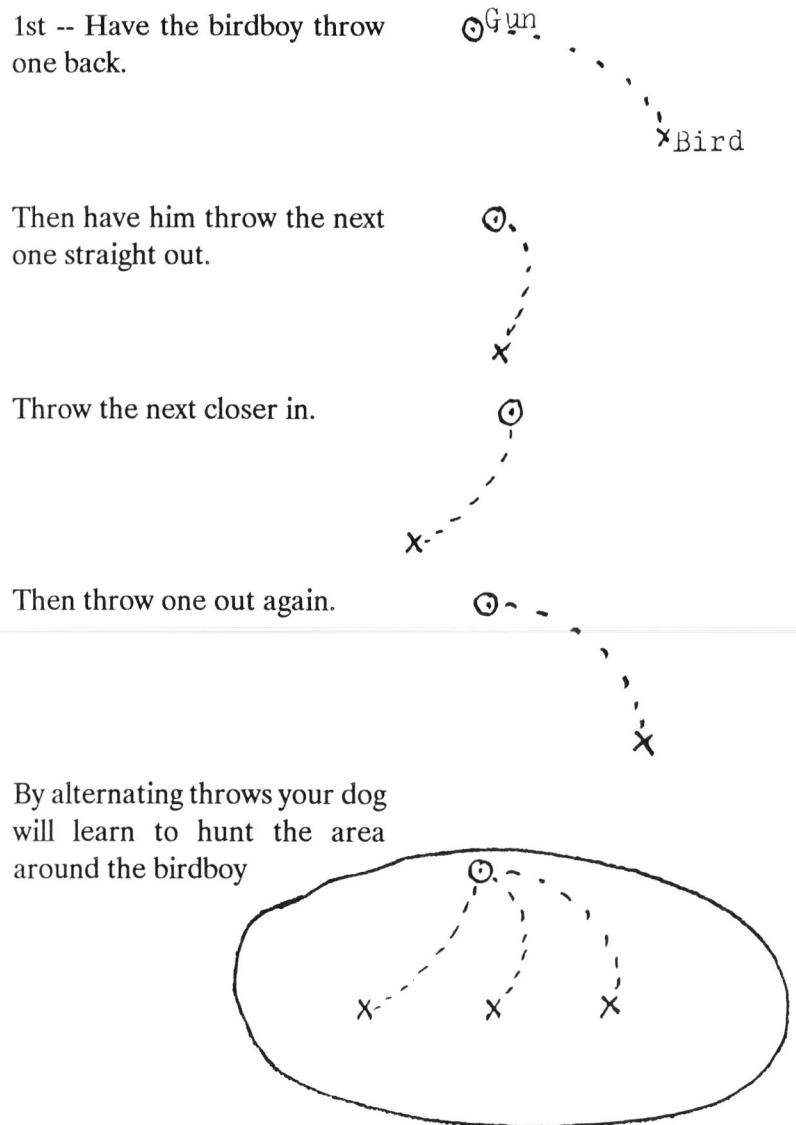

Melinda Snow shows how to use the insulated wire to remind a dog that has creeped to get back at heel.

This tripod has a Retrieve-R-Trainer attached. It can be fired by remote controls from nearly one mile away. The sleeve over the T bar represents the birdboy.

RETRIEVE   *Medcalf*

Melinda is holding the "foot long horseshoe" that is hammered into the ground and used for a stake.

The "breaking strap" shown at right has one end looped around the wrist. The other end goes around the dog's neck and through the small loop in the middle. The end can be held by either hand, and released only when the dog is sent for the bird.

Melinda is holding a bird in a sock. Use the same sock that you used for the puppy to introduce him to birds. The old sock will give him confidence. After several retrieves with the sock, the pup will probably pick up the bird without the sock.

These training sessions usually start out with a bull session at the local coffee shop.

Step back as the dog is coming to heel....

then step up as the dog turns to sit.

Take the dummy, and don't forget the "good dog."

RETRIEVE   *BIRDS AND SINGLES*

To teach a dog to hold a dummy that he has dropped, put pressure on his upper lips (against his teeth) and cram the dummy back in his mouth.

The instant the dummy is in his mouth release the pressure...and tell him "good dog."

Birdboys in action. Bryan, Texas 1986

Flat coat Retrievers can also play this game.
Ch Wingmaster's Beauford with owner Mary Yong.

NFC AFC San Joaquin Honcho

B. Jan. 23, 1973

Sire: FC AFC Trumarc's Raider Dam: Doxie Gypsy Taurus

Owner, trainer, and handler: Judy Weikel Aycock

1976 National Retriever Champion-youngest dog to win a national championship

National finalist 4 times-74 open all age points 68 amateur all age points

Honcho had a very distinguished all-age career; which included 2 double-headers, one national championship, and a national finalist 3 other times. Shortly after his sixth birthday he was retired from competetion. To this date, he has sired 42 titled dogs, more than any sire in the history of retrievers. Included in his progeny are 9 who were national finalist, 1 national derby champion, and the 1984 National Amateur Retriever Champion, NAFC-FC-AFC Trumarc's Zip Code. This great dog, at age 15, has been retired as a stud, and is enjoying his latter days, as he has for years, in command of his masters.

NAFC-FC TRUMARC'S ZIP CODE with owner, trainer, and handler JUDY WIEKEL AYCOCK

REX CARR seated, RICK ROBERTS standing. Preparing for 1984 National Championships

RETRIEVE *BIRDS AND SINGLES*

"FIELD TRIAL DOGS HUNT TOO"

FC-AFC HONCHO'S HARVEY HIGH POCKETS with DR. ED AYCOCK

Left-
NAFC-FC TRUMARC'S ZIP CODE with his son FC-AFC TRUMARC'S CLOUT

RETRIEVE *Medcalf*

FC-AFC KIZZIE'S ITSIE BITSIE with trainer, handler DANNY FARMER. Owned by MIKE PARKS

NAFC-FC TRUMARC'S ZIP CODE

SCHULER BOOKS

One of the Midwest's
Largest and
Most Complete
Bookstores

Over 75,000 Titles

517-349-8840
1-800-347-8841
FAX 349-8088

2075 W. Grand River Avenue
Okemos, MI 48864

CHAPTER 7

INTRODUCTION TO WATER

I could never understand why people make such a big deal out of a dog going into the water. Nearly all them are natural swimmers. You don't have to give them swimming lessons. I said "nearly all of them." I have had a few dogs on my place that got off to a bad start. My daughter used to let her dog "Hanna," play in the yard sprinkler at home. Hanna loved to chase the water and bite at it. When she was brought to me for training, she ran down to the pond, jumped in and started splashing and snapping at the splashes until she slowly worked her way into deep water. She ignored all requests by me to come back. After forty five minutes she became exhausted. She was getting lower in the water, and while I watched, she slipped out of sight. I kicked off my boots and jumped into the pond to save the dog. For weeks after the rescue I kept a long rope on the dog when there was water around. This dog apparently could not swim. She developed a habit of splashing water and just didn't make any headway. When I threw a dummy into the water and sent her for it, she leaped into the water and started splashing her way to the dummy. Before she got to it, she decided that splashing was more fun than retrieving, and I had to pull her out. I didn't waste a lot of time with her after a week or so of that. My daughter took the dog home with instructions to "keep her away from that blasted sprinkler."

Several months later we gave Hanna a refresher course on "fetch it up," and then sent her into the water for a short retrieve. I had a long nylon line on her so that could I get her out of there if she resorted to her old habit. She went the short distance to the dummy and retrieved it. I gave her a lot of praise, and tossed her another just a little farther out. She retrieved it, and started jumping around to get me to throw another. After a few more throws, I put her up. The next day I went through the same procedure. She retrieved with enthusiasm, and seemed to have forgotten about chasing the splashes. Even so, Monica never lets her out while she is watering the lawn.

Other dogs that I've had would start out splashing with their front feet, but apparently were trying to keep their head out of the water. Once they got the dummy in their mouth they would swim very well. If you have a pup that splashes with his front feet, let him drag six feet of rope when he swims. Sometimes that will help. Be in a position to get him in case the rope gets tangled in something. With a dog or puppy that has never been in the water, I start in a shallow pond. With hip boots on I wade out in shallow water and let the pup follow. I encourage him by clapping my hands and calling. If the dog doesn't come to me I wade around for a while and just let him watch. I'll try again the next day. Crossing a creek with the pup following is good way to get him into the water.

When the pup is "fetchin it up" pretty well on land, and starts jumping around barking at you to throw something, toss a white bumper into shallow water. After a couple of shallow water retrieves, gradually work him into deeper water. When the dog suddenly realizes that he is in swimming water, his desire to get the dummy will overcome his apprehension of swimming...if he doesn't have more than a couple of feet to swim for the dummy. After he discovers that he can swim, it's just a matter of building confidence. Don't try to make an Olympian out of him yet. Keep the water retrieves short, and not over four or five at a session.

During the initial water training, throw the birds or dummies so that the dog doesn't have to enter the water at an angle. Angle entries into the water at this stage of training will tempt the dog to become a bank runner. The dog should form a habit of going straight into the water to the bird and swimming straight back with it. You can have the dog run from as far back as you want by starting close to the bank, and moving back as before (in land singles).

HURRY UP METHOD

There are other ways of introducing a dog to water. A young friend of mine was going with me to his first field trial. I had my two dogs and he brought his six months old Chessie pup that was entered in the puppy class. Somewhere along the way Lester mentioned that his dog had never been in the water.

"What: he's never been in the water?"

"No Sir, but I'm sure he'll do O.K. He does real well on land."

Well, I wasn't so sure. Some of the judges set up seventy five to one hundred yard water retrieves that could be tough for a ten or twelve month old dog. For a baby that has never been in the water it would be nearly impossible. I hated to see this kid suffer the embarrassment that was almost inevitable, but starting a puppy in water is a time consuming process.

The next morning we were up before dawn. I drove out to a swampy area that we had seen from the highway the day before and pulled as far off the road as I could.

While I put on an old pair of tennis shoes, I told Lester to let his pup out. I fished around in a box of training equipment and got out a thirty foot piece of line with a snap on the end.

Now the Chesapeake Bay Retriever has a slightly oily coat that keeps his skin from getting wet when he is in the water. Cold weather divers wear a "wet suit" that keeps them warm in cold water. I didn't have either one, and I shuddered just thinking about what I was getting ready to do. This was late November and the water temperature was in the low forties. I was going to give Lester's puppy a crash course in water retrieving. We didn't have much time. The field trial was scheduled to start at 8:00 A.M., less than two hours away.

RETRIEVE INTRODUCTION TO WATER

I snapped the thirty foot lead on the pup and Les and I gave him a refresher on "fetch it up." I walked out and threw a few short marks for the pup, one at a time. When the pup picked up a dummy Les would give a light jerk on the line and encourage the dog to hustle back with it. After three or four of these short retrieves on land, I then took the end of the line and waded out twenty feet into the dark, stinking swamp. While I stood shoulder deep in the water, Les heeled his dog about eight or ten feet from the water and threw a white plastic dummy right in front of me. On the command "back" the pup ran down to the edge of the water and hesitated. I immediately pulled the slack out of the line and kept on pulling. Every time the pup tried to turn and go back, Lester would tell him to fetch it up, and I would turn him back to me with the rope. When the pup finally reached me I put the dummy in his mouth, gave him a "good dog," and sent him back to land. Lester shouted encouragements all the way, and lavished him with praise when he came out of the water. I waded to the end of the line and we went through the routine again. The third time, the pup took to the water without any help from me. One more retrieve and we left for the field trial grounds.

I made a quick change on the way and was still shaking when we arrived. The pup took a second place in the trial and drew some nice comments on his work. I overheard one judge tell the other "that little brown dog needs a little work on his land retrieves, but his water work was great." I also drew some comments, but they didn't have anything to do with retrieving. Well, so much for the slow introduction to water.

PROBLEM:

After several days of wading out in a pond, I still can't coax my dog into the water.

SOLUTION:

First of all, pick a day when there is not much wind, so the water won't be rough. Also I prefer to start a dog out in fresh water. If you have tried, unsuccessfully, for several days to coax your dog into the water, resort to something a little more forceful. Snap a leash on the dog and wade out into shallow water. When the dog pulls back, or resists, just ignore the struggle and keep on going. Once he gets in deep water he'll stop struggling and start swimming.

PROBLEM:

When my dog gets in the water he swims around and plays, and refuses to come to me.

SOLUTION:

Attach a long line to the dog and let him go into the water. After a few minutes call the dog. If he doesn't respond immediately, drag him out of there as fast as possible. Give him a refresher course on "here," and, with the line still attached, let him go back into the water. After a few minutes, call him to you. If he doesn't respond, jerk him out of there and repeat the "come here" lesson. Continue this until you are sure the dog understands what is wanted. If he continues after a week or two, consider a new dog or consult a professional.

CHAPTER 8

STRAIGHT LINE TO THE BIRD

If you plan only to hunt your dog, and are not interested in field trials, a straight line to a fall is not too important. The main thing is for your dog to mark the bird down, get to it as fast as he can and bring it back to you. If you are planning to get a Working Dog Certificate, or run in any type of field trial or hunting tests, it is necessary to teach your dog to take a straight line to the bird. Dogs are required to go through heavy cover, water, and over logs. The modern day field trial is a game of sorts, that shows how well a dog can be trained. Dogs will be required to retrieve triple and quad-ruple shot or thrown birds. Sometime the gunners will disappear after they shoot the bird, leaving nothing but the terrain to help the dog to remember where the bird fell. They will be required (in some stakes) to take directions from the handler out to "blinds," or hidden birds that may be three hundred yards out.

The new "hunting tests" will also have "blinds," and multiple marks, but the retrieves will not be as long. The hunting tests are set up to duplicate hunting situations. Handlers, as well as gunners wear camouflage, and dogs may be required to retrieve from boats and elevated duck blinds. So, for the "field trial" dog, or dog that will run in "hunting tests," a straight line to the bird is important.

NO CHEATING

To teach a dog to run straight to the bird, walk him over the terrain that you want him to go over. When he is going out to the bird don't let him run around, or "cheat" the tough cover. Don't let him run the bank around a pond. Make him take a straight line to the bird, come dells or high water.

To teach a dog to run straight to a fall you need to start early. Bad habits are always tougher to break than they are to prevent. Go back to the method of walking the dog through cover to the area where the dummy will fall before you send him. Any time he starts to avoid the rough spots, or run the bank, snap a short leash on him as before and walk him through the cover again. After walking him out, go back to the place where he went astray, or got off the line, and send him from there. If he does O.K. from there, move back closer to the start and run him through it again.

THE QUICK WHISTLE

To teach a dog to take a line through water, across a point of land, or through a channel, start the training on a small pond. Start at the edge of the water. Throw a dummy out about fifteen feet and send the dog. It is important that you throw the dummy straight out from the bank. Remember, don't throw it so that the dog has to go in the water at an angle. When he returns with it, throw another a little farther out. Keep throwing the dummy farther out each time until you finally have him going most of the way across. The instant the dog reaches the dummy blow a "come in" whistle. Most handlers use a long and two short whistles. Blow the whistle the instant the dog reaches the dummy. Get his attention on coming back. You don't want to give him time to think about running the bank or going somewhere else.

Once the dog starts back to you with the dummy, quit blowing the whistle. I see people blow their whistle constantly the whole time a dog is returning. They do it to encourage the dog to keep coming, but what they accomplish is the dog learns to ignore the whistle. If a dog hears a whistle blowing all he time, it won't have any more effect on him than a radio with the volume turned up high. Give him a loud "come in" whistle when he reaches the bird, and when he is coming to you, stay off of it. In training, you can encourage the dog by clapping your hands and shouting encouragements. If he starts to turn to the side or stops, then get after him again with the whistle. I said "in training clap your hands." If you are in a field trial just use your whistle. If you yell or clap your hands in a trial the judges may construe that as an intimidating gesture and drop you from the competition. Remember to keep the lessons short. Don't wear the dog out on this or he will be looking for a place to get his feet on the ground. Let him make several retrieves and then go to something else. Try to make the dog enjoy coming back to you with the dummy. Don't be too hard on him for dropping the dummy when he comes out of the water and stops to shake. If he does, go to the edge of the water while he is swimming back, and when he gets five or six feet from you, start walking backward, clapping your hands and encouraging him to keep coming. If he drops it, just go to him and put it back in his mouth. Get him to hold it a few seconds. Make him hold it while you both go back to the starting line.

RUNNING THE BANK

Now that you have the dog going across, or most of the way across, get a helper on the other side of the pond. Have the helper stand off to one side of the line that you are sending the dog on. Instruct him that you want the dummy to land on that same line. Have him yell to attract the dog's attention, and throw a dummy half way across the pond. Send your dog as before and encourage him to bring it back. Have the helper throw another, closer to the opposite edge. Keep working the dog across and up the opposite bank. When the dog picks up the first dummy that is thrown on the other bank, he is probably going to run around the shore with it. A dog doesn't have to be too smart to figure out that it is much faster by land than by sea. Now is the time to stop bank running.

When you have worked the dog across the pond, station a helper on each side of him to discourage the dog from running around the bank. If the dog starts to come around the bank, a helper should catch the dog by the collar and lead him back to the point where he would have entered the water. Now you shout encouragement

RETRIEVE / STRAIGHT LINE TO THE BIRD

for the dog to cross the water. Instruct the helpers to be easy with the dog. Your trying to teach the dog to come back through the water, not discourage him from retrieving.

If you are training without any helpers, work the dog across the pond as before. Throw each dummy a little closer to the other side until you have the dog going all the way across. If the dog picks up the dummy and starts around, instead of through the water, run around and intercept him. Take him back to the proper place (where he should have entered the water), tell him "stay," walk back and call him to you. Go through this until he tires of being dragged back, and eventually he will decide to swim across. When he does, let him know that is what you wanted all along. Hug his neck, pat him on the chest or whatever, but don't fuss with him about dropping the dummy to shake water, not heeling properly, or anything else right now. You have just reached a big milestone with your training, and want that dog to know that your happy about what he has finally done.

PROBLEM:

My dog runs around heavy cover or obstacles no matter how many time I walk him through them.

SOLUTION:

With the dog at heel, walk out into the middle of the heavy cover, or wade out into the water, and send the dog from there. If he is in the middle of the rough stuff he can't possibly avoid it. Make him return to you and send him again. After a few retrieves from the heavy cover, start moving back a little at a time to the original starting point. Come back to the same place the next day and have someone throw a mark where it was before. With the dog on a leash, send him for the dummy with "fetch it up," or "back," and jog along with him to make the retrieve.

When you and dog get back to the line, praise him. Do that two or three times, and then try sending him alone. If he takes the cover, make a big fuss over him and let him know that was what you wanted all along. This may sound like a lot of work on your part, and it is, but if you don't teach a dog to go straight to a fall early in his life, it will create problems later when you start hand signals.

RETRIEVE *STRAIGHT LINE TO THE BIRD*

This eleven month Chessapeake shows lots of enthusiasm...

...so let's back up the hill and see how he does from there.

RETRIEVE

Medcalf

The Golden Retriever is the "Glamor Dog" of retrievers. At right is Mistfield's Top Billing.

"Willie is not just another pretty face. He will be a credit to the "Goldens" that pick up birds for a living.

Owner G.F. Medcalf is the one on the left.

CHAPTER 9

BY LAND AND SEA

When a dog has to go in the water and out on the opposite bank, it is called an "in and out." Sometimes a dog will have to go through water, across a strip of land, and through another body of water to retrieve a bird.

To teach your dog "in and outs," find a pond that has a long point of land that sticks out into the water. The object is for the dog to go through the water, across the point of land, through the water on the other side of the point, and up on land again to pick up the bird.

With your dog on a leash, wade across on a straight line to where the bird will fall. Toss a duck on the ground and leave it. That will help him remember the spot. Then walk the dog back to the strip of land. The first retrieve will be made from there. Have someone throw a bird in the area of the one that you left on the ground, and send your dog. After he retrieves that one, throw him another. As he is returning with the second bird, wade back to the original starting line and encourage him to come to you. When he retrieves that one, give him a lot of praise, and throw him one more. This time he will have to cross both strips of water to get the bird. He will probably go all the way to the bird this time, because he has already been there twice. If he hesitates at crossing the strip of land, or the second body of water, give him a little encouragement. Tell him "fetch it up." If he doesn't go on across, wade out to the strip of land and try to drive him across. If that doesn't work, start over. From the strip of land, heel your dog and have your bird boy throw another bird or dummy in the same place as before. Send your dog, and if he doesn't go, snap a leash on him and drag him across and get him to pick up the bird. Make the dog "stay" while you wade back across the first body of water, and then call him to you. After you and that dog go back and forth several times, he will know what you want him to do. If he still refuses to go all the way, put him on a leash and drag him over to the bird, force him to "fetch it up," and then drag him back. Give him a "good dog" when you get back, even though you had to force him all the way. When your patience starts to wear thin, put him back in the kennel and try again tomorrow.

PROBLEM:

My dog goes across the first water, but won't go any farther.

SOLUTION:

1. Go back and start from the beginning, Make sure the dog knows what you want him to do. If you go through the procedures every day for three or four days and still don't get results, go back to something that the dog can do well for a few days. Let him get his mind off of the "in and out." After that, take him back to a different place and start all over. Try not to lose your temper with the dog.

PROBLEM:

My dog will go across and pick up the bird, but then he runs farther away and won't come to me.

SOLUTION:

It sounds like you may have put a lot of pressure on your dog, and he is not coming back to you because he doesn't want to be punished. Throw him a bird about ten or fifteen yards out in the water and send him for it. When he gets to the bird, encourage him to come back by clapping your hands and shouting encouragements. Don't hassle him about heeling, or holding the bird. Throw him a few more, each one a little farther out. Try to keep him happy while he is retrieving these, and gradually work him across the first body of water. Quit while he is doing something right. Come back the next day and do the same thing. After a few days he will regain some of his confidence and start training again.

2. Sometimes a young dog will go across and then not want to get in the water again to come back. If this seems to be the case with your dog, put the long nylon cord on him, and then send him for a bird. If he hesitates on the way back, pull him to you with the nylon line. He probably will drop the bird, but pull him back anyway. After he has been forced back a couple of times, he will probably come back on his own...with the bird.

CHAPTER 10

DECOYS

If you hunt waterfowl, or plan to enter your dog in any type of field trial, your dog will have to retrieve through decoys. When your pup shows enthusiasm for retrieving in water, that's the time to start.

Put six or eight decoys on the bank. Spread them out in two groups, ten feet apart. Let your dog tag along with you while you are putting them out. If he starts to pick one up, just tell him "no" and put it back. Don't make a big deal out of it, just let him know that you don't want him to bring decoys to you. After you get set up, throw a dummy for your dog. Throw the dummy so that the dog has to run between the two groups of decoys to get to it. Start close to the water and move back five or ten feet after a couple of retrieves. Keep throwing from farther back until the dog is going thirty feet or so before he passed the decoys. If he stops to investigate, or picks one up, don't let him bring it to you. Walk out to the dog, yell "NO!" and take it away from him. Then move a little closer and start over.

After your dog becomes accustomed to the decoys on the bank, move some of them out into the water. Go through the same procedure as before. Gradually move them farther out until you have them all in the water. When the dog is marking the dummies well, and ignores the decoys, move the starting line farther back. Add more decoys to the spread. Put them out so the dog has to swim through them to get to the dummy. Before long, the pup will think that decoys are just part of the landscape.

I was invited to hunt with a guy that had taught his dog to bring the decoys in after a day's hunt. He thought that was clever, and bragged about his dog being a strong swimmer.

It was cold on the lake that next morning, and I had just poured us some coffee when a pair of whistlers come streaking past. We both dumped our coffee in an effort to get off a quick shot, but neither of us scored. The man's dog ran out of the blind and jumped in the water. He made a beeline for the nearest decoy, and spent the next five minutes trying to drag one back. Swimming in circles, he got tangled in the decoy lines and couldn't get loose. As the dog was going under, my friend ran down and jumped in to save him. Ordinarily Don was a fairly good swimmer, but he failed to consider the burden of swimming with hip boots, and a shell vest. Fortunately, the water was only five feet deep. I made a dash for the boat that we had hidden in the brush, and Don kept the dog from drowning till I got to him. We cut the tangled anchor lines loose and then made it back to shore.

We built a big fire, and stood around trying to dry out.

"I can get in the boat and get those decoys that are drifting off while you're thawing out." I said.

"To hell with them," Don said through chattering teeth. Then he looked contemptuously at his dog. "I've already lost over a dozen on account of that stupid dog."

"How's that?" I asked.

"That's the third time this year I've had to go in the water and cut him loose." Then he added, "sometimes I don't think he'll ever learn."

Well, I like to use a few decoys when I am training, but I'm not sure my dogs are smart enough to retrieve them either.

SUNSHINE'S FLYING TIGER MH

Born February 2, 1983

Sire: FC/AFC CFC/CAFC CHESDEL CHIPPEWA CHIEF

Dam: FC/AFC ELIJAH'S SUNSHINE SALLY

Owner, trainer and handler: Bill Medcalf

"ACE" was in the first litter of Chesapeake puppies born that had Field Champion sire and dam. He was fourth dog of all breeds to earn the title MASTER HUNTER

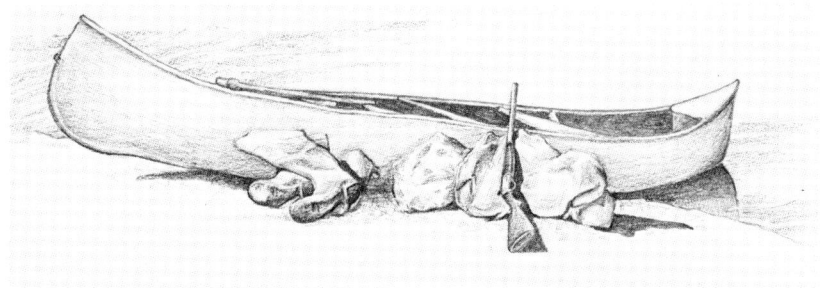

CHAPTER 11

WORKING FROM A BOAT

If you hunt waterfowl you should teach your dog to retrieve out of a boat. Start out with a canoe, or jon-boat, up on the bank about five feet from the water. Get in the boat with your dog at heel and throw a dummy in the water for him. After he retrieves that one, throw him a few more. Then move the boat closer to the water. Keep moving the boat until the dog is jumping into shallow water to retrieve. After he gets used to that, gradually work the boat farther out. When the boat is floating, and the dog is going out of the boat into deep water, you will have to help him back in the boat. If the gunnel of the boat is low enough for the dog to get his paws over, just hold your hand behind his head and let him push back against you to help him climb in. If that doesn't work, grab him by the collar, or the skin on his neck and pull him in. If you're working out of a boat that has a lot of freeboard, and the dog can't reach high enough, grab him by his front legs and pull him in.

PROBLEM:

My dog will not jump out of the boat into deep water to retrieve.

SOLUTION:

Go back to the shoreline and work him from there until he builds some enthusiasm. Then work him back into deep water. If he still refuses to go, gently assist him with one hand on his collar and one holding his tail. Don't heave him as far as you can, just help him over the side. When he gets in the water, encourage him to "fetch it up."

PROBLEM:

My dog goes out of the boat O.K., but when he gets the dummy he heads for the bank, and won't bring it to me.

SOLUTION:

1. Get your nylon line and snap it on his collar. Send him for a dummy. When he gets it in his mouth, call him, and gently pull him back. When he gets to the boat, take the dummy, and give him a lot of praise before you help him in.

2. If your dog still refuses to return, take him out in the middle of a big lake and throw him one. Let him swim around until he discovers that you have the only game in town. After he retrieves from out there a few times he may decide that coming back to the boat "ain't so bad after all."

Try not to lose your temper and pull him out of the water by his ears. What ever you do...give him a "good dog" while he is dangling there.

CHAPTER 12

DOUBLES ANYONE?

A double is when two birds are shot in rapid succession. The dog should mark both birds down, and retrieve them, one at a time. Any retrieving dummy or bird that is thrown or shot for the dog is referred to as a "mark."

The first bird thrown is normally called the "memory bird." The dog will have to remember where it fell while he retrieves the second bird thrown, called "the diversion."

RETRIEVE *Medcalf*

When you start with doubles, find a fence with a big gate, or a hedge row, or something to separate the two areas where the dummies will be thrown. Open the gate and heel the dog in a position in line with, and facing the fence that will separate the two marks. First, throw a dummy on the left side of the fence and send the dog. After he retrieves that as a single, throw the first mark of your double in the same place you threw the single, (left side) and hold the dog. That will be the "memory bird." With the dog still at heel, throw the second mark of the double on the right, or opposite side of the fence and send him for it. That will be the "diversion." After he retrieves the second bird thrown, (diversion) send him for the first bird that was thrown (memory bird) that you threw to the left. He should remember where it is because he has already been out there (to retrieve the single that you threw).

There are a couple of things that you should do to help the dog remember the second mark. As he is returning with the first, turn and face the next one that he is to retrieve. When he comes to heel, he will automatically be lined up in the direction he has to go. Another thing is to take a few steps toward the second mark as you send him. That will help him get started off in the proper direction. After he has moved a couple of yards he will have the fence between him and the first mark to discourage him from changing his mind and switching. In training, it is always a good practice to run your dog on the first bird as a single. This applies whether the dog is old or young, and whether you are going to run him on a double, triple, or quad. Remember, you are training the dog. Retrieving a single before you throw a double will help him remember. Help him succeed in what you want him to do. Testing will come later, on the field trial grounds or on the marsh. After the dog understands the doubles separated by the fence, go to the open field.

You're going to do the same thing with a double in the field that you did with the fence, except without the fence to separate the marks.

If you are using birdboys, have them go out about fifty yards from the (starting) line. Position them so that there is a least a ninety degree angle of separation. The wide angle will help discourage the dog from switching. Instruct your birdboys that you want the dummies to land outside of that ninety degree angle. Also have them yell to attract the dog's attention each time just before they throw. The one on your right will throw to your right, and the one on your left will throw to your left. With both throwers in the field, have the one on your left throw a dummy. Send the dog for it. In the early stages of training, run the dog on the first bird as a single two or three times before running him on the double. After the dog has retrieved the left bird as a single several times, throw it as the first bird of the double. Then with the dog at heel, throw the right, or diversion bird. Send the dog for the diversion as before. Take a few steps toward the fall to help get him started. As soon as the dog picks up the dummy, give him a "come here" whistle and encourage him to come to you. Don't let him start for the other (memory) bird. If he stops or starts to switch, clap your hands, call him, blow the whistle and do everything you can to get him headed your way. When he gets back with the dummy, take the dummy and then send him for the memory bird. Take a few steps with your hand out in front of him to help him get started in the right direction. If he tries to go back to the same place that he's just been, run toward the memory bird and try to draw him back in the proper area.

If training alone, you will do things about the same except that you will throw the dummies yourself. Be sure and have a wide angle between the marks. Dogs have more of a tendency to break when you are throwing dummies from the line. Hold the dog with the breaking strap until he is steady.

After the dog becomes proficient on short doubles, start making the retrieves longer. Vary the angles and the direction of the throws. You will know a dog is ready for more difficult retrieves when he starts to take a quick glance over where the other bird fell while he is returning with the first one.

PROBLEM:

The most common problem when starting a dog on doubles is switching. A dog that goes to the area of a fall, hunts and fails to find the bird, then leaves the area to hunt for another has switched. If a dog drops a bird he is retrieving and goes to hunt for another, that is a switch.

SOLUTION:

If your dog has gone to the area of a fall, hunted for the bird, and then decides to go to the other bird, hustle out to the area that he left and encourage the dog to come back. When he comes back to the area, keep him hunting there until he finds the bird. After he brings it to you, set the double up again and start over.

Let's say that your dog starts out for the diversion, or last bird thrown. Half way there he changes his mind and switches. Try to stop him before he gets to the other bird, and bring him back to the spot where he left the line. Make him stay at the spot where he changed course. You may have to tie him to a stake, or get someone to hold him. Then go (without the dog) to the area that he cut across and throw a temper tantrum. Kick dirt, stomp, thrash the weeds, whip the ground, and yell "NO! NO! NO!" while you are doing it. Then calmly walk back over to the dog and send him for the bird. Go back to the starting line, and run the dog on the same bird again. Chances are, he'll go where he is supposed to. When he starts thinking about switching, he'll remember you raising hell out there and avoid that area. If he switches again, throw another tantrum. If he still switches, I'd swarm all over the dog and give him an idea of what he's been missing.

PROBLEM:

After my dog has had a long hunt in an area without finding the bird, he will leave the area.

SOLUTION:

1. Sometimes a dog will leave an area where he has been hunting to clear the scent from his nose. He will then come back into the area and continue the search for the bird. When a dog does leave the area after a long hunt, give him a chance to come back. If he doesn't return after a minute or so go out to the area and encourage him to come back and hunt for the bird.

RETRIEVE   *Medcalf*

PROBLEM:

My dog retrieves the first bird O.K., but refuses to go for the second one.

SOLUTION:

1. When a dog refuses to leave the line, it is usually because he doesn't understand what you want him to do, or has been harshly punished for making a mistake and is afraid to make another.

When he retrieves the first bird and then will not go for the next, the dog probably doesn't remember the second bird. Before you send him on a double, throw the memory bird as a single several times. Then throw the double. When he makes the first retrieve, don't hassle him about holding the bird, or heeling properly. Just take the bird and send him for the next as soon as you can. Take a few steps to get him started. When he comes back, run the same double a couple of more times.

2. If the dog refuses to go the first time, it's probably because he is afraid of being punished for making a mistake. Throw some short singles for the dog and try to restore his confidence. Clap your hands and encourage him to retrieve. Don't fuss over the little things such as sitting, heeling, or holding the bird. When he is eagerly going after the bird again you can gently start enforcing the formalities. It is important to always wind up a training session with something the dog can do easily. Some dogs can naturally mark birds and remember them better than others. Be patient, I've never seen one yet that couldn't learn to count to two.

RETRIEVE   DOUBLES ANYONE?

PROBLEM:

The dog brings the first bird back, drops it close by, and then takes off for the other.

SOLUTION:

1. This dog has a strong desire to retrieve. He is so anxious to go back and get another bird that he short cuts the formalities. The eager dog is fun to train, but don't let him develop bad habits. When this dog comes back with the first bird, have your leash or breaking strap ready. As he approaches the place that he drops the bird, step out and quickly put the strap around his neck. Make him heel. Put your hand in front of, and over his head, and then send him for the second bird. He should quickly learn that you want him to come to heel before going for the second bird. And then to go only on the command "back."

PROBLEM:

My dog is so anxious to retrieve that he creeps out several feet in front of me when the bird is thrown.

SOLUTION:

1. A dog that creeps will develop into a breaking dog if not brought under control. When a dog creeps out in front of you, back up two or three steps and then yell "HEEL!" He'll be surprised when he realizes how far out in front of you he is. Don't walk back to the original line. Heel the dog back to you. If the dog stays, and doesn't creep, send him from there. If he creeps up again, back up some more. Keep moving the starting line back when the dog creeps. He will realize that creeping is causing you to move back, and that he doesn't get to go for the bird until sent by you. Run him from where you backed up to. If the dog continues to creep after a few training sessions, you may need to resort to a more positive correction.

You can make a simple tool to help you teach the dog not to creep. You'll need a round piece of wood twelve inches long and two inches thick, and a piece of stiff, single strand electrical wire eight or nine feet long. The electrical wire has insulation that will keep the wire from cutting the dog. Twist one end of the wire tightly around one end of the wood and the other end of the wire around the other. Stretch it out into a long "U" shaped loop.

When you heel your dog and signal for the bird to be thrown, have the handle of the loop in your hand with the loop above and behind you. When the dog starts to creep, tell him "HEEL!" and reach out with the loop and give him a sharp jerk back. He probably won't see the wire swing over his chest, but he will think about it the next time he starts to creep. After a few times with this loop, most creeping problems become a thing of the past.

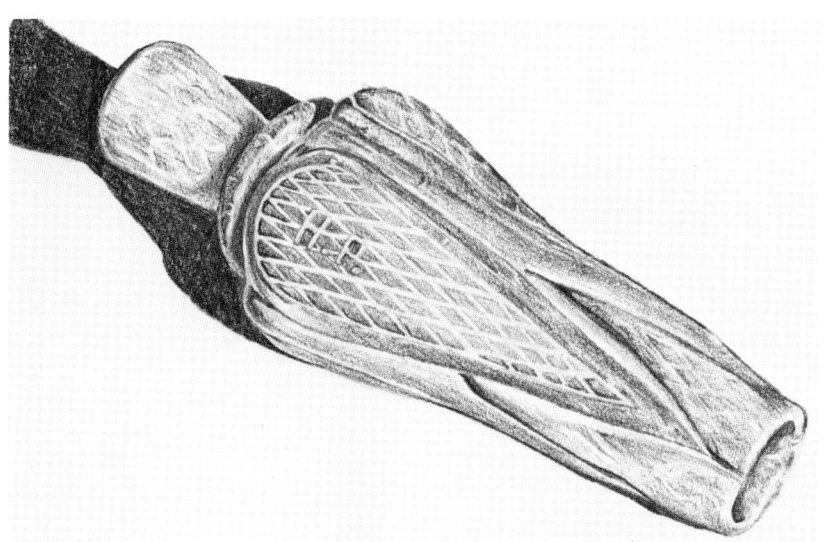

CHAPTER 13

TAKING A "LINE"
(Direction from the handler)

The word "line" crops up often in dog training. First there is the starting line, then the straight line to the bird, and now the term, "take a line" comes in to the picture. If you attend a field trial you probably will hear the term used along with "blind." "The dog took a good initial line to the blind," or "He lined the blind." In a field trial, a "blind" is a bird that is planted, or hidden before the handler brings his dog to the starting line. The dog doesn't know where the bird is, so the handler has to direct the dog to the bird with hand signals. In a hunting situation, a "blind" would be a shot bird that the dog did not see fall.

To retrieve a blind, whether hunting or in a field trial, put the dog at heel facing in the direction of the blind. Put your hand over and in front of the dog's head, aiming, or pointing to the bird. Send the dog with the command "back." The dog should go on the "line" that you have sent him on until he finds the bird. If he gets off the line, stop him with a long blast on the whistle, and handle him back on line, and then back to the bird. Handling will be covered in the next chapter. Before you teach your dog to handle, he has to learn to "take a line."

To teach your dog to "take a line," find a straight road or path two or three hundred yards long. For this part of the training use white dummies. They are easy for the dog to see. Lay out six or eight white dummies, fifteen yards apart, in a line down the road. Walk the dog out and show him the first dummy. Go back to the (starting) line with the dog at heel and place your hand over the dog's head, pointing toward the dummies. Give the command "back" and take a few steps toward the first dummy. That should get the dog started. If he retrieves the dummy, just toss or drop it behind you, line him up and send him for the second one. The dog will probably go to where the first dummy was, see the second one, and go pick it up. When he returns, send him the same way for the third. He should run to where he just picked up the second one, spot the third one and go for it. He will eventually become confident that he will find something if he just keeps going.

The next day set up the line of dummies on the same road, only put them farther apart. Have the first one out about thirty yards.

When you send your dog, he will probably take a line to where the first one was the day before, take a quick look, and then continue down the road. If he doesn't seem to know what to do when you try to send him for this thirty yard "blind," go back to the original pattern. Lay out the first dummy so that he can see it and let that lead him to the next.

I have had people tell me that teaching a dog to take a line down a road will cause them to run any road they cross later on. Especially when running across diagonally. To prevent that from happening, start your dog lining on a road as before, then move over in the field parallel to the road, then move farther away and run another. Soon the road will be out of the picture, and the dog will be taking the line that you give him with your hand. After a few days of this, set up similar lining drills out in the field, over creeks, across roads, and through heavy cover.

PROBLEM:

The dog picks up the first dummy, but on the next retrieve he goes back to where the first one was and stops.

SOLUTION:

1. Go to the spot where the first dummy was picked up and send him for the second one from there, just as you did from the first point. When he picks up the (second) dummy, put the first two dummies back out and start over. It won't take long for the dog to be taking long lines down the road.

Another "lining drill" that I use is called the "wagon wheel." With the dog at heel, drop several dummies in a pile. This pile will be

RETRIEVE Medcalf

the "hub" of the wheel. Let the dog see the dummies. Then walk the dog fifty yards or so out one of the "spokes" of the wheel. Line him up on the pile (at the hub) and send him for one. Put your hand over his head, give him a "back," and take a couple of steps to get him started. When he retrieves a dummy, get him at heel and walk around the "rim," over to a different "spoke." As you start to move around the circle, just let the dummy slip to the ground where you sent him from (at the first spoke). Move around to the next spoke. Line the dog up on the pile of dummies and send him as before. When he comes back with the dummy, let it slip to the ground as you did with the first. Move on around the circle doing the same thing until you get four or five dummies out. Now take the dog back to the hub, to where the pile of dummies was. Line him up on the spoke that leads to the first dummy that you dropped out on the circle and send him. This is going to be more difficult for the dog, so when you send him, take a few steps with him toward the dummy. You may have to go most of the way with him. Always get the dog to return to the starting point, or the hub, with the dummy. Line him up for the next one (second spoke) and do the same thing. Continue this until he has picked up all of the dummies. Remember to turn and face the next spoke when the dog is twenty or twenty five yards (on the return) so the dog will automatically be facing in the right direction when he comes to heel. He will learn that you are facing the next one. That will help him remember multiple marks later on.

PROBLEM:

The dog refuses to go, acts as if he does not know what you want.

RETRIEVE   *TAKING A "LINE"*

SOLUTION:

The dog probably does not know what you want. Take a few steps when you send him. Keep your hand over his head or in front of him and keep saying "back." If necessary, go all the way to the dummy with him saying "back" all the way out. When he does pick up the dummy, hustle back to the starting line and praise him for the retrieve.

PROBLEM:

The dog runs to the first dummy in the line and then leaves it to pick up the second.

SOLUTION:

I wouldn't fuss over this too much. After the dog picks up the close ones, he will settle for the first one that he comes to. This drill is used to build confidence in the dog. He has to believe that there is a bird or dummy out where you are sending him.

CHAPTER 14

LINING IN WATER

A retriever must learn to take a "line" in water as well as on land. When you start lining in water, try to find a long shallow pond that has some weeds, or plant life growing in it. When you lay out the string of dummies, tie a clothes pin on each dummy and attach the dummy to a weed with the clothes pin. That will keep it from drifting away. When the dog makes the retrieve, the clothes pin will pull loose from the weed and come back with the dummy.

To lay out a "line" in deep water, attach an anchor weight to the clothes pin to keep in in place. Snap the clothes pin on the dummy so that the dummy will pull loose when the dog grabs it.

PROBLEM:

When Sport is returning with a dummy through weeds, the clothes pin tangles and jerks the dummy away from him. He acts as though I pulled it away from him, leaves it and comes back to me.

SOLUTION:

1. Any time the dog returns without the bird, hustle him back out and make him "fetch it up." You don't have to be rough on him because something jerked the dummy out of his mouth. Just wade out to him as he is returning and encourage him to keep trying. If he can't get the dummy to come loose after a few tries, go pull it loose from whatever it is hung on and then let him retrieve it.

A dog learns to pull very hard to break a bird or a hung up dummy loose. Not long ago my seven year old granddaughter and I put on a retrieving exhibition for a children's fair. During the last part of the show, a drunk staggers up and ask if one of the dogs can retrieve his wife, who has drifted out in the lake. After a short conversation between Melinda and the dog, Melinda sends Ace, my two year old Chesapeake, to make the rescue. He swims out to the seventeen foot boat, grabs the bow line, and tows the distressed lady back to shore.

Now I've never towed a boat with my teeth, but the jerk when the slack comes out of the line must be somewhat astonishing. In comparison, I think pulling a clothes pin off a limb would be easy. I trained Ace to tow the boat by trying a retrieving dummy to the bow line. I shoved the boat a few feet out into the water and then sent him to retrieve the dummy. The first few times, the weight of the boat would jerk the dummy out of his mouth. Each time I would encourage him to go back and get it. About the fourth time, he grabbed it and held on. After a couple of days of that, I removed the dummy and made a large back-splice in the end of the bow line. With a little duck scent sprinkled on, the splice worked fine as a replacement for the retrieving dummy. Now I think Ace would tow a barge up the river and never look back. I can hardly wait to see what he does at the next field trial where the gunners are sitting in a boat.

This shows a line of dummies on the mowed "cross."

For markers, use a long piece of wire with a red ribbon tied to it.

When starting on doubles, use a fence to seperate the two marks. The fence will help the dog learn not to "switch."

RETRIEVE   *LINING IN WATER*

To keep dummies from drifting... attach them to water plants with clothespins.

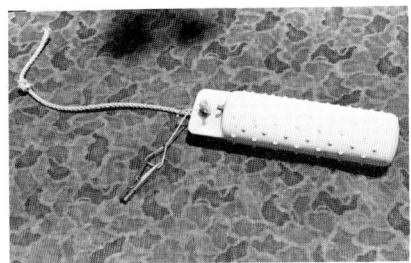

Then lay out a line in the water and send the dog...

...just as you did on land.

CHAPTER 15

HANDLING

THE BASEBALL DIAMOND

There are two parts in learning to "handle." The dog has to learn whistle and hand signals, and the handler has to learn what signals to give the dog, and when to use them.

Before you start to teach your dog to take hand signals, there are a few tools you will need. In addition to the "foot long horseshoe" and nylon line that was mentioned in the Problem section of Yard Breaking, you will need a hammer to drive the "horseshoe" into

RETRIEVE   *Medcalf*

the ground, a whistle, and three retrieving dummies.

Start a concentrated program to "stop and sit to the whistle." Put a leash and choke chain on your dog. Walk him around, and every few minutes give a loud, single blast on the whistle, jerk on the leash, and give the command "sit!" You want the dog to learn to sit the instant he hears the whistle. Give him a short lesson on this several times a day until he starts to respond instantly. After that, you can take the leash off of him and do the same thing. Let him run around while you take a walk, hit your whistle and yell "sit." Clap your hands together when you tell him to sit and demand instant response. Now lets go to the baseball diamond.

We are going to use an imaginary baseball diamond to teach the dog to take hand signals. In addition to "stop and sit" to the whistle, he will learn four more signals. The first two will be "over" left and right. The third will be "back," and the forth will be a "come in closer" signal.

Most of us know that a baseball diamond has home plate, first, second, and third base that form the shape of a diamond. In the center of the diamond is the "pitcher's mound."

Drive the "horseshoe stake" into the ground at the pitcher's mound with the top sticking up two or three inches. Walk your dog out to the pitchers mound. Slip the snap on the end of the nylon cord through the horseshoe and snap it on the dog's collar. With the nylon cord in hand, give a "sit" blast on the whistle, and a reinforcement jerk on the nylon line. Walk back to "home plate," and hold on to the cord (that has been slipped through the horseshoe and is snapped onto the dog's collar). Now you can hold the dog at the pitcher's mound while you are standing at home plate.

Give a "sit" blast on the whistle, and when the dog is watching, toss a dummy out to first base. Hold your dog for a few seconds, and then release the line. With your right arm extended out to your side, yell "**OVER**" and take a few steps to your right. The dog will probably run over to retrieve the dummy, and the nylon line will slip through the horseshoe and not restrain him. After your dog retrieves the dummy, walk him back to the pitcher's mound. Have him sit, with a blast on the whistle and snap the long line on him as before. Walk back to home plate, and toss another dummy to first base. If the dog tries to retrieve before you send him, hold him with the line. Give him another blast on the whistle to reinforce "sit," and then send him "over." Extend your right arm as before. It may not be necessary to move toward the dummy after you have thrown a few for him, but any time he hesitates, help him out by taking a few steps in the direction of the dummy.

After you have thrown a couple to the right, give him one to the left. Do the same thing you did before, only extend your left arm and take a couple of steps to your left as you yell "over." Alternate left and right "overs" until your dog starts to anticipate your commands. At this point your dog is probably not associating the extended arm with anything. He is turning in the direction that you threw the last dummy, and is waiting for the command "over" to release him.

So far, the dog should not be having any trouble. You have the line to keep him from "breaking" before he is sent, and he has been retrieving the dummy that he has just seen thrown. Now we are going to complicate things a little.

Walk your dog out to the pitcher's mound and snap the line on him as before. Go back to home plate and throw a dummy to first base. Now throw another dummy to third base. Most dogs will turn and watch the last dummy thrown. In this case it would be the one at third base. With the dog looking toward third base, give a single blast on your whistle to get his attention, extend your right arm and give him a loud "over" toward first. The dog will probably try to take off for third. If he does, stop him with the nylon line, then give him the "over" to first again. This time extend your arm out and take several steps toward first base to help get him going in the right direction. When he does go to first and retrieves the dummy, give him a lot of praise. Walk him back out to the pitcher's mound and return to home plate. You still have a dummy at third base, but the dog has probably forgotten about it.

Give a "sit" blast on your whistle and throw a dummy to first base. The dog will be anticipating going after it, so send him to third base. Use exaggerated movements...left arm outstretched, and take a few steps in the direction you want him to go. If it is necessary, go all the way to the dummy that you are sending him after. Keep your arm outstretched and repeat the command "over" as you go. After a few days of this your dog will start to watch you to see which way you are going to send him. When he starts watching you, it's time to start teaching him to go "back."

Walk your dog out to the "pitcher's mound" as you have been doing. From "home plate," blow a "sit" whistle, and throw a dummy over the dog to second base. After you throw the dummy, blow another "sit" whistle to get the dog's attention. While he is watching you, raise your arm straight up, give the command "back" and take a few steps toward the dog. Keep your arm up high and make a pushing motion as you walk forward, as if you were driving the dog back. Repeat the "back" lessons until the dog is responding to your hand over your head and the voice command "back," without you taking any steps toward him to get him started.

When you think that your dog understands "over," and "back," accompanied by the hand signals, start alternating the commands. Be sure and use the horseshoe and line, and remember...be patient. You are teaching the dog...not testing. It is important that you walk your dog out to the pitcher's mound every time. If you give him a "line" to the pitcher's mound and stop him with a whistle, he will learn to run out about twenty five yards, anticipate the whistle and stop. That is called "popping," and is a bad habit, and hard to break. At this stage of training send the dog to retrieve a dummy other than the one you just threw. If the dog starts to go for the wrong dummy, stop him with the nylon line, not the whistle. Use exaggerated movements. Extend your arm in the direction you want him to go, and don't be shy about walking rapidly toward the selected dummy to get him started. After your dog becomes fairly proficient at left and right "overs" and "backs," you can add "come in closer" to his repertoire. To teach your dog "come in closer," walk the dog out to second base and make him "sit." Return to home plate and blow the "sit" whistle to get his attention. Toss a dummy toward the pitcher's mound. The signal that you are going to use for "come in closer" is a series of short toots on the whistle, accompanied by your hand held at the side of your leg, down about knee level. Give the "come in closer" signal, and when the dog gets to the dummy give him one long and two short blasts to pick it up and come home with it. You will notice there is a difference in the signal to "come in closer," and the signal to "come in." The "come in" means just that, to come all the way in. The "come in closer" signal is telling the dog that he is too far out, and needs to look closer in for the bird.

Now you have exposed your dog to all of the necessary signals for handling. He should be able to "take a line," stop at the long blast of the whistle, take signals "over," "back," or "come in closer." Most dogs can become proficient at playing "baseball" in a few weeks of "two a days." The longer the time between training periods, the longer it will take your dog to catch on. The problems crop up when you leave the ball diamond and start handling your dog to longer blinds. That is what we are going to do next.

RETRIEVE *HANDLING*

Seven year old Melinda Snow shows how to send a dog "OVER."

This shows the dog responding to the hand signal.

RETRIEVE

When sending a dog "back," hold your hand up as if stopping traffic and take a step toward the dog.

This is the response that you should get from the dog.

RETRIEVE   *HANDLING*

Melinda shows the proper way to send a dog "back." Hold your hand above and out in front of the dog's head like a gun sight. Don't make a chopping action with your hand, just tell the dog "back" and let him run out from under your hand.

When you send a dog "over," use your whole body. Remember...the dog has to see these signals from a couple of hundred yards out.

RETRIEVE

Medcalf

This sequence shows Melinda and "Ace" playing baseball. Walk the dog out to the pitcher's mound...

then return to home plate...

and give him an "over" to third base.

"Gee I hope he does this the right way."

RETRIEVE   *HANDLING*

This Lab is being held by the "foot long horseshoe."

As seen in these photos, you can hold the dog and move away from him with the horseshoe stake.

THE CROSS PATTERN

To teach your dog to handle at longer distances, you need an open field two or three hundred yards long. It may sound unrealistic to say that a dog will be making three hundred yard retrieves in a hunting situation. but think about the bird that glides a long distance before he collapses. Or think about some of the tests set up by field trial judges. Think about the hunters in the next blind. If they don't have a dog, you may be able to get your limit of ducks without ever firing a shot. If your dog learns to "take a line" for three hundred yards, and will respond to your whistle that far out, you will be ready for just about any situation that comes up.

The set-up that we are going to use to teach the dog to handle at longer range is called the "cross pattern." You will need twelve dummies, and three markers. The markers are just a stiff wire two or three feet long with a piece of red surveyor's tape or ribbon tied on one end. The red is easy for (most of) us to see, but dogs do not see red well. This imaginary cross will be about two hundred yards long. The "arms" of the cross will be about fifty feet down from the top, and spread out about fifty yards wide. Stick one of the markers in the ground at the top of the cross. Put the other markers at the ends of the arm of the cross.

With your dog at heel, walk out and drop six of the dummies in a pile. This pile will be at the top of the cross. Now put three dummies by each marker at the ends of the cross arm. You and your dog walk midway down the cross, about one hundred yards or so from the pile that you put at the top. This will be the starting line for the exercise.

Heel your dog facing the top pile. Give him a line with your hand over and in front of his head, and send him to the top pile with the command "back!" He should go directly, on a line to the dummies. Remember to hit the "come in" whistle the instant he gets to the dummies. Don't give him time to think about anything but "bring it back." After you take the dummy and toss it behind you, line him up and send him again. Just before he gets even with the cross arms, give him a long "stop and sit" blast of the whistle. When he stops, and is looking at you, give him an "over" to the left. Again, hit the "come in" whistle the second he picks up the dummy. Line him up and send him again. This time you want him to go back to the top pile. The next time stop him at the cross arms and send him "over" to the right. Alternate between the top pile and over left, and the top pile and over right. If you send him to the top pile every other time, it will usually keep him running all the way out. If you stop him short too often, he will anticipate the whistle and slow down before he gets to the dummies at the top of the cross. After your dog picks up a couple of dummies from this distance, move the starting line back. You can gradually move the line back until he is handling from two hundred yards or more.

THE DOUBLE CROSS

After your dog is working the "cross" very well, add another arm to the cross, This one will be thirty five yards closer to the starting line. With the "double cross" you can stop your dog short, stop him farther out, or let him go to the pile. Be sure that you let him go to the pile more often than you stop him and send him "over." This will keep him from anticipating, and stopping before he hears the whistle.

PROBLEM:

I don't think that my dog will ever catch on to the hand signals. If I don't let him go for the last dummy thrown, he will not go at all.

SOLUTION:

Some dogs catch on quicker, and have more enthusiasm than others. I have not seen a retriever yet that could not learn to play "baseball" at close range. It sometimes takes more patience and time than I think it is worth, but if you stay with the program long enough, he'll learn it. If your dog is having trouble with handling at close range, I doubt if he will ever be a good worker at two or three hundred yards. If you're concerned about your dog being stove up from arthritis, or developing hardening of the arteries before he catches on, you might consider making a pet out of him and get another prospect for retrieving.

PROBLEM:

My dog will take a line out about twenty five yards, stop and wait for me to give him another command.

SOLUTION:

This problem is called "popping". It is usually caused by the handler repeatedly sending the dog on a line, stopping him a short distance out, and giving him an "over." In training, you should give

RETRIEVE   HANDLING

your dog a lot of long lines mixed in with short ones so that he doesn't anticipate the short whistle and "pop." I mentioned in the "baseball" training that you should always walk your dog out to the pitcher's mound. If you sent your dog on a "line" from home plate, and stopped him with a whistle at the pitcher's mound throughout the training, he would develop a habit of stopping that may take years to break.

NEAR SIGHTED DOG

PROBLEM:

A friend of mine told me that his dog was "near sighted." He said his dog could not see past seventy five yards.

SOLUTION:

1. This is a common ailment, but it doesn't have anything to do with the dogs eyes. My friend had been using a "Retrieve-R-Trainer" to throw dummies for his dog. The "Retrieve-R-Trainer" is an excellent tool. It uses a nail gun blank to fire a dummy seventy five yards or so out into the field. My friend had been shooting dummies for his dog all year long, and the dog developed a habit of going seventy five or eighty yards, and no more. In the dog's mind, there was no reason to go farther out because he had never retrieved anything farther out. A dog will build up a mental "wall" if he is only sent to retrieve at a certain distance. He won't run any farther than he has been going throughout training. If you have had someone in the field two hundred yards out throwing birds for you, your dog will accept that as a reasonable distance and hustle on out there. If you have a Retrieve-R-Trainer, don't shoot dummies from the line all of the time. Have someone walk out in the field and throw birds, or dummies whenever you can recruit some help. That will keep your dog from building a "wall." I have my Retrieve-R-Trainers mounted on tripods. I set them up as far out in the field as I want, and fire them by remote control.

If you train by yourself, you can do essentially the same thing by making your dog sit at the starting line while you walk out into the field and throw the dummy. If necessary, use the horseshoe stake to make him stay. After you throw the dummy, walk back to your dog, line him up and send him just as you would if someone else had thrown for you. If your dog has trouble marking the fall, help him the same way as before. Tell him to "hunt em up," and walk as far as necessary out toward the area. After he picks that one up, go back and do it all over again. Stake him out and throw one in the same place. He will probably do better the second time. If he still has trouble, shorten the distance to the fall by moving the dog closer to the area that the dummy will land. When he does O.K. from there you can move farther back.

2. Go back and read the section on "taking a line." Lay out a string of dummies. Space them thirty yards apart, all the way out to the pile at the top of the cross. Send your dog for them one at a time, and gradually work him out two hundred yards or more. The next day do the same thing with him, only make him go a little farther to pick up the first dummy. Each successive day make him go farther for the first one. He has to be confident that when you send him, there is something out there to bring back. If he still can't see past seventy five yards after you have done all of that...take him to an optometrist.

RETRIEVE *HANDLING*

PROBLEM:

My dog will go on a straight line for one hundred yards or so. Then he starts to wander, and acts like he can't hear the whistle.

SOLUTION:

When you give a dog a "line" in training, put the bird or dummy that you are using for the "blind" downwind of the starting point. If you run your dog into the wind he may not be able to hear the whistle, (or your screams), as well as he could if he were downwind of you.

It is common for dogs to "turn you off" when they get a couple of hundred yards away (My wife accuses me of the same thing). They seem to think that the farther they are from you, the more they are on their own. When your dog does this, and he will, you should hustle out in the field and "set him straight." Let him know that he still has to respond, no matter how far out he is. When you have to run out in the field to get a dog's attention, give him a "whistle drill" just like you did in yard breaking. If you have to go after him again, don't take him back to the starting point. Go about half way back and run him on the blind. Then go back to the original line and run him again.

There are a lot of things that will take a dog's attention away from you. He may see an old white plastic jug, or a sun bleached piece of wood that he thinks is the dummy that you are sending him after. Sometimes there are smells that will draw them off the line. They have to learn to ignore the distractions and stay on that line. If you run 'Ol Sport down for ignoring you often enough, eventually he will start to listen. And just think...the exercise you get isn't nearly as boring as jogging.

PROBLEM:

When I send my dog on a long "blind," sometimes he will go over the hill out of sight. What should I do?

SOLUTION:

There is a saying in field trial judging: "Out of sight, out of control." Here is what they mean. If you are trying to "handle" your dog to a blind and he is out of your sight, you don't know what the dog is doing. You also don't know what signals to give to direct him to the bird. In a situation like this, the judges in a trial will probably ask you to "pick up your dog." That means that your dog has been dropped from the competition. When you are in training or a field trial, and your dog looks like he is going out of sight, **STOP HIM**!! Give him a long blast on the whistle and when he stops call him in closer, and then try to handle him to the bird.

Some judges use the "out of sight, out of control" theory in tests that are not "handling" tests. In my opinion that is wrong. Sometimes a dog will overrun a bird, go out of sight for a few seconds, and then come back and pick up the bird. A dog might leave the area of the fall to clear the scent from his nose, and then come back and hunt in the proper area. I ran Topaz in a trial in Canada that had a judge that believed in the "out of sight" theory. Topaz went for the last bird in a triple, that had been thrown just down from the top of a hill. She ran over the hill, and out of sight. One of the judges was a friend of mine, and probably wanted to give me the benefit of any doubt. When Topaz came back over the hill a few seconds later and picked up the bird, the judge eased up to me and said, "I could still see her tail, couldn't you?" I just smiled, and accepted his "gift."

I was told a long time ago..."don't pick up your dog until the judge tells you to."

Most of the time I listen to advice the pros give me, but not always. If you let your dog spit in your eye at field trials and get away with it, he will soon become "trial wise." He will learn that he can get away with things in a trial that he would be punished for in training.

I ran Ace in another trial in which the judges were definitely not believers in the "out of sight" theory, except for handling tests.

The derby test was set up on a long narrow pond. It was to be a double that consisted of a short memory bird, thrown about thirty yards out into a tiny island of cattails. The next bird would be thrown across the pond at a wide angle from the first. This was a very simple test for an almost two year old derby dog. Well, when I went to the "line" with Ace, there was a couple of men about two hundred yards from us. They were standing on a dam directly beyond the little cattail island. Both had on white jackets, and were talking very loud. When I realized that they were not birdboys, I asked the judges, "What's going on with the people standing on the dam?"

One of the judges looked up and yelled **"HEY! GET OUT OF THERE! WE'RE HOLDING A FIELD TRIAL HERE!"**

"Can I take my dog off the line while you clear them out?" I asked.

"Just stay where you are. They're leaving now."

This wasn't fair to Ace. The way he was watching the men, he probably thought this was going to be a triple, and one of the birds would be thrown up on the dam. In a field trial the judge is king, so Ace and I stayed. After the men cleared out I called for the birds. First they threw a bird to the island. Next was the bird across the pond. I lined Ace up for the "cross the pond" bird and sent him. He retrieved that one and was staring intensely at the place where the two men had been. When I sent him for the duck in the cattails, he swam as hard as he could, past the island, and on to the dam. He came out of the water, and made a quick search. Then he went over the dam...out of sight.

We all waited. Everyone was was watching the dam. After five minutes went by, I started getting nervous.

"Where the devil is that stupid dog?" I muttered to myself. Then I thought "don't pick up your dog unless the judge tells you to."

Two more minutes went by. I wished that I had put my return address on him. I may never see him again.

"Would you like for me to pick up my dog?" I quietly asked.

"Let's just wait a couple of minutes more." the judge replied.

About that time, Ace came bounding over the dam and jumped in the water. He made a beeline for the duck in the cattails, and brought it to me. I took the bird and handed it to the judge without even looking up. Ace usually knows when he has done something I don't like, and comes back with his tail dragging. He was wagging his tail now, and acting as if he had just won the nationals.

Ace was called back to run the next series, in spite of the disappearing act. I supposed it was because of the excellent job he had done up until then. He had an outstanding job on the last series, and wound up with a fourth place. I didn't think he deserved it, but I didn't turn it down.

Later that day I was standing around talking, when Carrol Hay came by. Carrol and Ian Hay were running the trial, and were staying in a camping trailer that was parked close to the dam.

"What the heck is the matter with that dog of yours, eh?" Carrol asked.

"Nothing. Some days he's just not as smart as others."

Carrol laughed "This afternoon he came running over the dam by the trailer eh?, and picked up one of the ducks that I had laying on the ground to dry. I yelled 'fetch that duck up here', and he brought it to me. Then he picked up another and I called him to me again. I put the ducks up on the trailer where he couldn't get to them. Ace kept bringing me ducks, and after he retrieved all thirty five ducks, he ran back over the dam and jumped in the water. I looked over the dam and he was swimming hell bent for the other end, where they were having the water test."

The mystery of the disappearing dog had been solved. Ace had probably set a record for the number of ducks retrieved in any field trial...and I didn't even give him a pat on the head.

In this sequence I prepare the dog with my hand over her head...

...send her with the command "back!"...

...stop her with the whistle on the first cross bar...

...Then send her "over" to the left.

RETRIEVE *HANDLING*

This time I let her go all the way to the top of the cross.
Send a dog to the top at least twice as much as you stop him with the whistle. That will help keep him from "popping," or stopping before you blow the whistle.

This time I stopped her at the top arm of the cross...

...and send her "over" to the right...

RETRIEVE *HANDLING*

The dog must "deliver to hand."

I take the dummy after she comes to heel...then tell her she's a "good dog."

AFC ARTIC SUNSHINE SALLY FC/AFC ELIJAH'S SUNSHINE SALLY FC/AFC S&S SUNSHINE MEG with owner, trainer, handler STEVE PARKER

One bird in hand and two to go.
CAROL ANDERSEN and Duel Champion FIREWEED'S JASMINE

With Steve and Carol on the grounds even a second place is hard to get.
At right is the author and SUNSHINES FLYING TIGER MH (ACE) ACE is the one on the right.

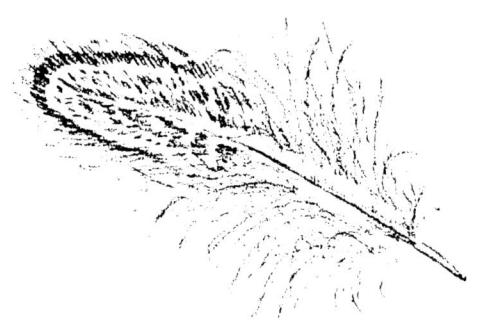

CHAPTER 16

QUARTER AND FLUSH

If you hunt upland game, or enter the Master Class in a hunting retriever test, your dog needs to learn to "quarter and flush," and "stop at flush."

Quartering is when the dog runs back and forth in front of you as you walk through a field. The dog flushes a bird, and stops when the bird flushes.

Start out by teaching your dog to stop at flush. With your dog on a leash, or breaking strap, walk around a pond. Throw a dummy while you are walking and fire a blank pistol while the dummy is still in the air. If your dog tries to break and run after the dummy, yell "**WHOA!**" and give him a hard jerk on the leash. Make him stand, or sit for a few seconds and then release him with "fetch it up." After he makes the retrieve, start walking again and do the same thing. When your dog learns to stop at the throw and shot, take him off the leash and do the same thing. Tell him "**WHOA!**" after you shoot, just to remind him that he still can't break and run after the dummy. After the dog is stopping at the flush and shot real well, it's time to go to the field.

You used the command "hunt 'em up" in training to get your dog to hunt in an area that he left. Now you will use the command to teach him that you want him to quarter in front of you. He will remember the "hunt 'em up" lesson and start looking for a bird when you give the command.

Since most shotguns have an effective range of only forty five yards or so, teach your dog to hunt close enough for you to kill the birds that he flushes. If he is consistently flushing birds out of gun range, you would be better off without him.

Walk through the field, clap your hands and tell your dog to "hunt 'em up." Make him stay out in front of you. When he gets too far out, call him back in. Don't use your whistle, just talk to him. When he comes closer tell him to "hunt 'em up" again. Most dogs will quickly learn how far they can go, and will stay in that range most of the time.

As you walk along, throw a dummy and shoot, just as you did at the pond. The farther the dog is from you, the more tempted he will be to chase after the bumper. Pitch it out away from him, and don't hesitate to let him know that he is supposed to stop...until you send him. Practice with the dummies until your dogs gets the hang of it, and then try the same thing using dead birds. After the dead birds becomes "old hat," get someone to walk along with you and throw a live pigeon. Most dogs get very excited when you shoot birds over them, so you need to shoot a lot of birds if you plan to run in the hunter tests.

PROBLEM:

When I throw and shoot, my dog is so distracted by the gun that he forgets where the dummy landed.

SOLUTION:

Start by throwing the retrieving dummy in a pond. You can reassure the dog that everything is O.K., and he will still be able to mark the bird from the rings in the water. After he has had a lot of "throwin and shootin" he will probably do much better.

PROBLEM:

I'm having trouble keeping my dog from breaking when I throw a bird, or have someone shoot a flier.

SOLUTION:

1. Snap the nylon line on the dog and have someone shoot a bird. When the dog breaks for the bird, yell "**NO!**" as loud as can, and try to jerk him off of his feet. Do this often enough and he will probably catch on.

2. I use a homemade device that enables me to release a live bird by remote control. I put a quail or pigeon in the trap and work the dog to it from the downwind side. If my dog breaks when I release the bird, I don't shoot. If the dog holds, I kill the bird...sometimes. An intelligent dog will associate his stopping at the flush with the killing of the bird.

CHAPTER 17

TRACKING

Tracking is a skill that a dog needs to learn if he is going to run the Master Hunter tests. I don't mean that a dog will have to track desperados, or lost children. He will be required to follow the trail of a bird that has been dragged along the ground for a hundred yards or more, and retrieve the bird.

To get started on tracking, you will need three markers, twenty feet of nylon line, a ten foot pole, and a dead bird. Put your dog in a kennel, or someplace so he can't watch while you lay out the track. Tie the bird so that it dangles about three or four feet from the pole. Mark the starting point, and scent the area around it by dragging the bird back and forth. Drag the bird downwind through the grass for forty or fifty yards, make a ninety degree turn and go another forty or fifty yards. Untie the bird and leave it on the ground. Put a marker close to the bird, and at the place where you turned. These markers will help you remember exactly where the trail is. When you are dragging the bird, hold the bird out away from you so your scent doesn't get mixed in with the birds.

Attach the twenty foot line to the dog's collar and lead him to the scented area. Let him smell around the starting point for a few seconds, and then tell him to "go find it." I use "go find it" for the tracking command because it sounds different from "hunt 'em up." You want the dog to learn to follow the track, and not quarter back and forth. Keep the dog on the lead and keep saying "go find it." He will try to hunt for the bird, and when he does, just pull him in close to you and tell him "go find it." After you put him back on the trail a few times, he will start putting his nose to the ground and follow the scent.

Lay a track for your dog every day before you start training. Early in the morning the ground is usually cooler, more moist, and will hold scent better. Try to keep your scent as far away from the track as you can, and always make at least one ninety degree turn.

As the dog gets better at tracking he'll keep his nose to the ground instead of trying to find scent in the air. Run him on a track without the lead. If he starts to quarter just call him in and tell him "go find it" as before. Make the tracks a little more difficult. Put in more turns, or lay the trail across a log, or a creek. You can increase the difficulty by waiting a while before you run him on the trail. Any

RETRIEVE   *TRACKING*

time your dog starts to quarter instead of follow the track, put the lead on him and give him a refresher course.

CHAPTER 18

TRAINING TIPS

1. Teach your dog to run a straight line at an early age. That will make most of the other training easier.

2. If your dog cheats the cover, or runs the bank, stop him and make him do it the right way.

3. Be sure the dog can see the dummy or bird hit the ground. It is difficult for a dog to judge how far out a bird is when the bird goes out of sight behind a hill. Squat down and take a look from the dog's level.

RETRIEVE   *TRAINING TIPS*

4. Try to do things so that you are able to correct the dog if he makes a mistake. Example: Your dog is in the water and refuses to listen to you. You don't want to go in after him because you're wearing a new suit, and $400 cowboy boots. Results...the dog learns that he does not have to obey you when you are well dressed. (That's why we dog trainers sometimes look like we do).

5. When your dog quits hunting and starts to come back, or leaves the area of the fall, go out in the field and hustle him back to the area. Make him continue to hunt until he finds the bird.

6. If, for some reason, you and the dog cannot find a dummy, drop another one while the dog isn't looking and help him find it. The dog might get discouraged after a long hunt if he never finds anything to bring back. Try to make him successful.

7. Don't send your dog through an old mark, or old scent.

8. When training on doubles (or triples), throw the memory bird as a single before you set up the double.

9. Any time your dog looks like he is eating a bird, or starts to pull feathers, get the bird away from him in a hurry. Give him a "come here" lesson, and insist that he bring the birds to you without delay.

10. At times, training an animal gets to be frustrating. If you're having trouble with your dog, make sure he understands what you want him to do. See that there are no obvious distractions, such as paper blowing around, other people yelling at their dogs, or a poodle in a bikini.

11. You can undo a lot of training when you're angry. If you lose your temper, quit for the day. Dog training should be fun.

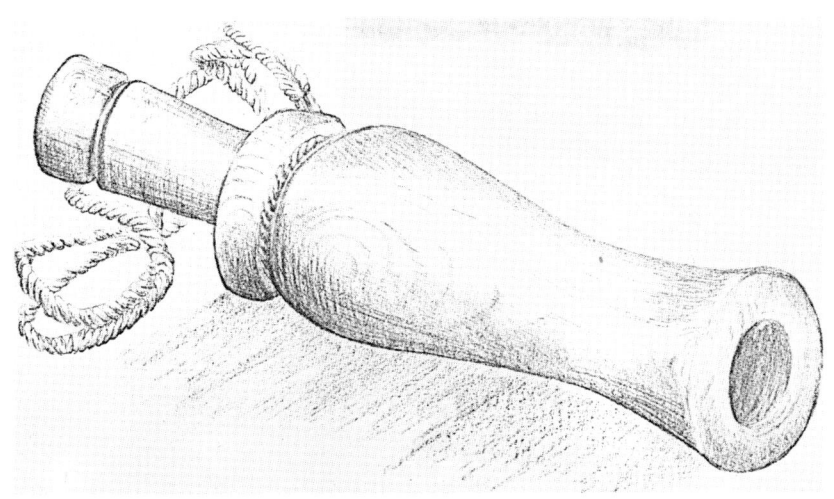

CHAPTER 19

HANDLING TIPS

There are a lot of things that handlers do that help their dogs...or cause them trouble. This is a list of some things you should know, and some things you should avoid doing.

1. The standard whistle signals that most handlers use in field trials are:

STOP!...One long blast on the whistle.

COME HERE...A long blast and two short toots. (Morse code letter "D".)

COME CLOSER...A series of five of six short tweets on the whistle with your hand held down beside your knee.

2. Don't blow your whistle while the dog is returning with the bird. A whistle blowing all the time will have about the same effect as "hard rock" music turned up high. Give him a "come in" blast to get him started, and then no more, unless he gets sidetracked and stops.

3. Wear a white jacket so your dog can see you. (In hunting test wear camouflage.)

4. Do not touch your dog while you are on the line. If your dog just did an outstanding job, wait till you leave the immediate area, and then show him that you are pleased with him.

5. When you go to the "line" in a field trial, show the dog the gunners, or birdboys, in reverse order from the way they will be throwing. Example: In a triple where the birdboys on the left will throw first, then the ones in the center will throw, and then the ones on the right, walk up to the line and heel your dog facing the ones on the right. Watch for the dog to show recognition, (his ears will go up when he spots them) then turn and heel the dog facing the middle gunners. When the dog finds them, turn and face the ones on the left. After the dog has seen all three sets of gunners, signal the judges that you are ready. With as little movement as possible, you have shown your dog all of the gunners, and are facing the first bird to be shot (The one on your left).

After they shoot the first bird, turn and face the middle gunners, When they have shot and thrown their bird, turn and face the ones

RETRIEVE   HANDLING TIPS

on the right. The dog will probably turn with you and be lined up on the last bird thrown. That is the bird you want him to retrieve first.

When your dog picks up the bird and is returning with it, turn and face the next bird that you want him to go for so that when he comes to heel, he will be facing in the direction of the next retrieve.

In the new "Hunting Retriever Test," the gunners are probably going to be wearing camouflage, or out of sight. Be sure the dog is facing the direction of the fall before you send him, then use your hand over his head to start him in the right direction. You are not allowed to "point out" the gunner's positions in hunting tests.

6. When you are going to handle your dog to a "blind," don't send him on a "line" until his body is lined up, and he is looking in the direction that you want him to go.

7. Be aware of the wind direction and terrain. Most retrievers don't like to run into the wind. If you're sending your dog on a "line" in a cross wind, allow for the possibility that he will drift downwind.

If you are "lining" him across a hillside, allow for the natural tendency of a dog to go downhill.

8. In a handling test, if you think your dog is going out of sight, **STOP HIM!** with your whistle. Then handle him back to the bird. If he goes out of sight he will probably be dropped from the competition.

9. Watch the "big boys" (pros) handle their dogs. You can see how they cope with different situations.

As you progress with the training, you will feel the satisfaction of comradeship develop with your dog. It will be a pleasure working with him, and seeing the happiness the dog gets from knowing what is expected from him and how to do his job well.

RETRIEVE *HANDLING*

There are always pretty girls at
field trials...

The author (right) with pros. Hank Tullis, and Mary Nell Gray.

What do you think of that last dog?

CHAPTER 20

THE HUNTING TEST

The "Hunting Retriever Test" is the new game in town, and it is the best thing to come along since "night baseball."

For years the only yardstick we have had to measure a puppy's potential for retrieving was the FC/AFC preceding the parent dog's name...providing the parent dog is a field champion. The WC, WD (working dog) titles issued by the breed organizations are usually not put on registration papers or pedigrees. FC/AFC titles are awarded only to the top field trial dogs, usually after years of expensive training and campaigning. Some of the finest dogs never see the field trial grounds, but have a lifetime of retrieving in the fields and marshes during the hunting seasons.

Hunting Tests differ from the conventional "Licensed Field Trials" in several ways. Field Trials are a win-lose situation. Your dog can take a 1st, 2nd, 3rd or 4th place and receive points toward a title. That's it. Even if there are seventy dogs in the competition only four will be in the money. In "Hunting Tests" every dog competes against a standard, not against other dogs. If your dog completes all of the tests, and does a nice job, he gets a ribbon...plus points toward a title.

There are three different levels of difficulty in the hunting tests. The A.K.C. (American Kennel Club) calls them Junior, Senior, and Master. NAHRA, (North American Hunting Retriever Association) calls them Started, Intermediate, and Senior, and the U.K.C/H.R.C. (United Kennel Club/Hunting Retriever Club) calls theirs Started, Seasoned, and Finished. No matter what you call the "hunts," they are all FUN!

The "Junior," or "Started" tests are single retrieves on land and water. Scoring is based on the dog's ability to "mark" the bird, his "style" on the return, and his willingness to deliver the bird to the handler.

The "Seasoned" or "Intermediate" tests are a little more difficult. They will have "double" retrieves and a "blind," and maybe a "diversion" bird thrown while they are returning with one of the birds in the "double." These tests are for dogs that have a hunting season or two behind them, or a little more advanced training.

The most difficult category is the "Master, or "Finished." Dogs that run this level are expected to mark and retrieve three or more birds (a triple), run 100 yard blinds, track wounded game, and quarter and flush upland game. They will usually have several "diversions," and may be required to work out a duck blind or boat.

All hunting tests are set up to duplicate hunting conditions. They use duck blinds, boats, decoys, duck and goose calls, and the judges and handlers wear camouflage. The handler will carry a shotgun, and in the UKC/HRC tests he will be required to shoot (blanks) at birds that are thrown. I was first introduced to the "Hunting Test" in 1983 in W. Swanton, Vermont. It was called the International Gun Dog Classic, and was similar to the Hunting Tests that are becoming so popular today, Since then the "hunting test" movement has spread over the country like a grass fire.

Hunting Retriever clubs are cropping up all over the U.S. The participants, young and old, are mostly people that do their own training. They are having a lot of fun meeting other families with a common interest...dogs.

Another group that has jumped into the middle of the "Hunting Tests," is the kennel owners that breed dogs for conformation. Their customers still want "show quality" dogs, but now some of them want dogs that can retrieve as well as look pretty. In order to satisfy their customers, the kennel owners are learning to train field dogs...and are having a lot of fun doing it.

Several people have told me that participating in the "Hunting Tests," is like having a license to hunt all year long. If you want to have more fun with your dog and "hunt year 'round," join a hunting retriever club.

You can get a list of clubs in your area by writing:

Hunting Retriever Club, Inc.
%United Kennel Club
100 E. Kennel Rd.
Kalamazoo, MI. 49001-5598

N.A.H.R.A.
P.O. Box 6
Stafford, VA. 22436

The American Kennel Club
51 Madison Ave.
New York, N.Y. 10010

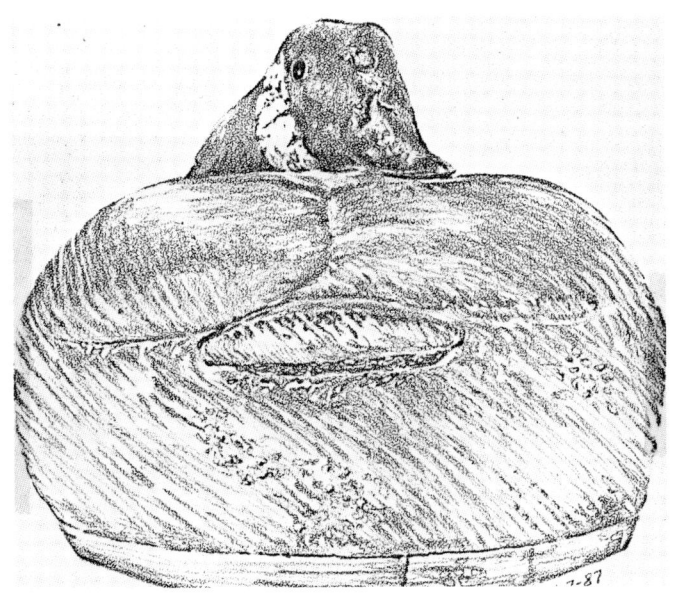

CHAPTER 21

SAMPLE TRAINING TESTS

Here are a few sample tests you can set up. When setting up a training test, place the gunners so the dog will run cross wind with the wind coming from the bird toward the gunner. That will help the dog learn to "mark" the fall.

If you run your dog into the wind, he will smell the bird long before he gets to it, slow up, and follow his nose. This will teach him to "hunt short," (not run all the way to the bird) instead of marking where the bird fell.

RETRIEVE   *Medcalf*

Start with singles. Set up tests so that you can increase the difficulty by moving the starting line back, or left or right.

When you run a double, set up the test, and run the "memory" bird as a single. Then run the double.

Generally, the tighter a test is, or the closer the angle between the marks, the more difficult the test. You can start a double, or triple with the "line" fairly close to the marks, then move the line farther back to make it more difficult. Moving the "line" to the left or right will tighten the angle between the marks, and also make one farther out than the other.

1. Instruct birdboys to keep all birds off the ground.

2. Have them throw each bird so that the dog can see it hit the water or ground.

3. Be aware of the wind.

4. Birdboys should stand quietly, facing where the bird landed after each throw.

5. Start with an easy test, and gradually increase the difficulty.

6. Start a young, or inexperienced dog on short, easy retrieves. As he gains experience, increase the difficulty by moving the starting line farther back, changing the angle, or running through a creek, ditch, or change in terrain.

7. Have the dog doing well on land before working in water. On land you are better able to correct mistakes.

5. Bird falls on side of hill.

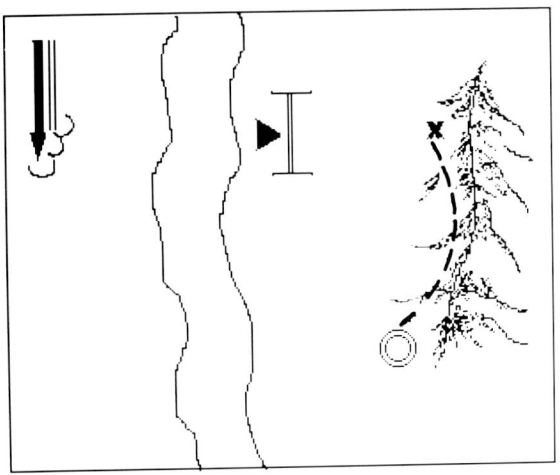

6. Dog crosses creek to pick up bird on hill.

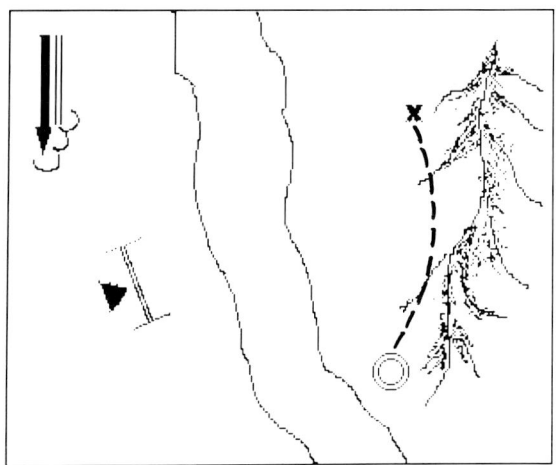

RETRIEVE   SAMPLE TRAINING TESTS

3. Longer retrieve---Dog has to cross road.
   <----------as far as you want---------->

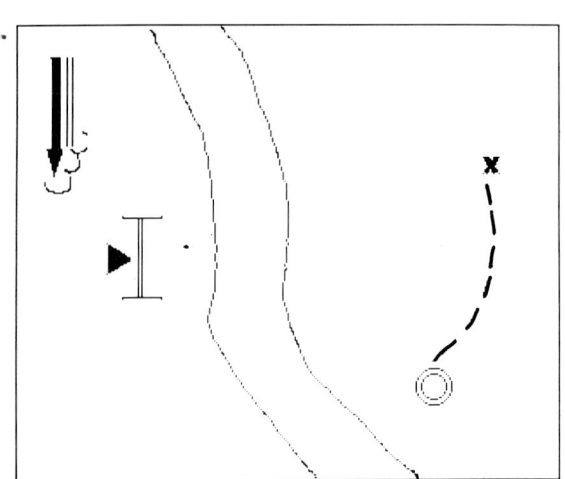

4. Gun is on near side of road---Bird lands on far side.

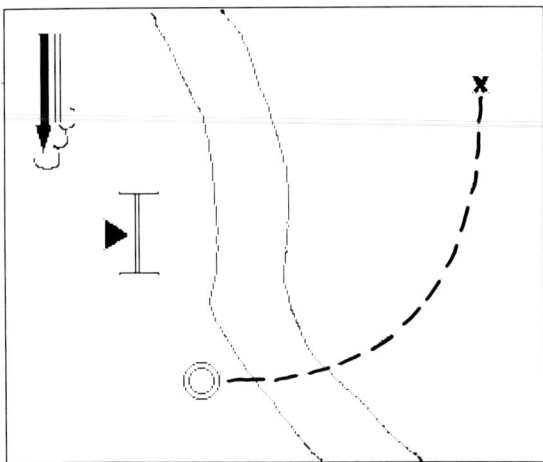

RETRIEVE   *Medcalf*

SINGLE

1. Set up the test.
2. Walk the dog through cover, water, etc., before throwing the first bird.
3. Make the first retrieve short, then increase the distance by moving the starting line back.

Here are some samples...

---

1. Single with no hazzards or diversions.

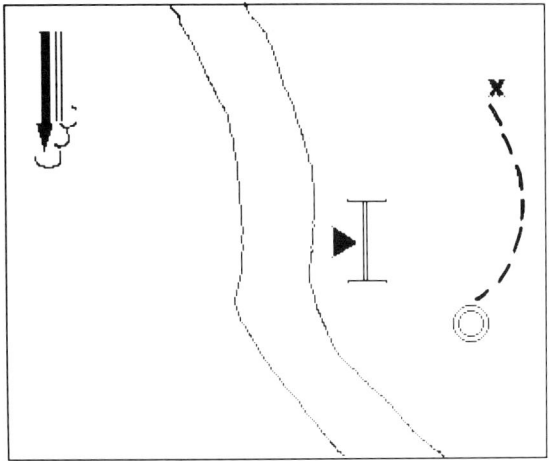

---

2. Dog has to cross a road.

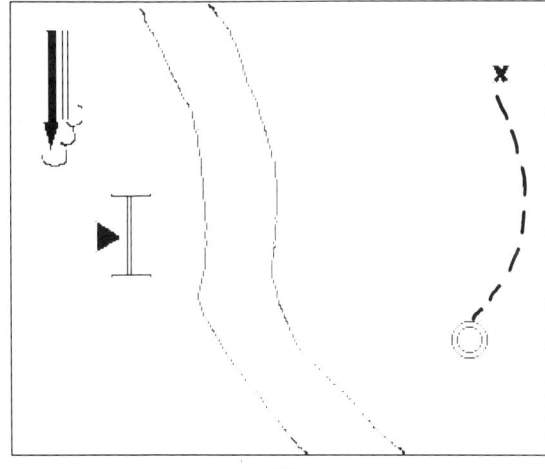

RETRIEVE   *SAMPLE TRAINING TESTS*

Set up training tests for young or inexperienced dogs so the wind is blowing from the bird toward the birdboy. Most dogs have a tendency o run to the birdboys, or gunners. Wind carrying scent from the bird will draw the dog away from the gunner and back to the bird, helping him make a successful retrieve.

Dog smells bird and is drawn away from gunners.

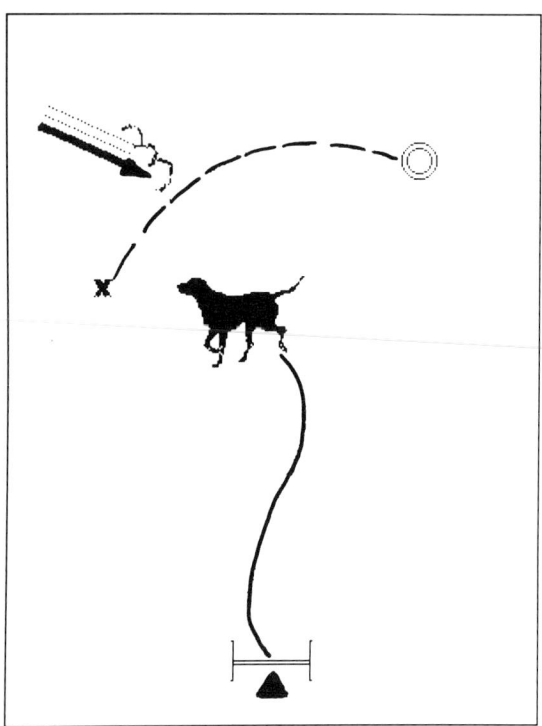

RETRIEVE   SAMPLE TRAINING TESTS

7. Downhill, across creek, up side of hill.

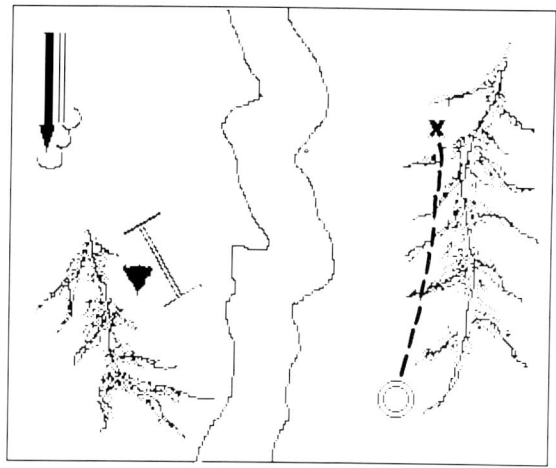

RETRIEVE

Medcalf

The wind can help a dog make a successful retrieve when distracted by decoys.

Dog smells bird and is drawn away from decoys.

RETRIEVE   *SAMPLE TRAINING TESTS*

8. Water singles.

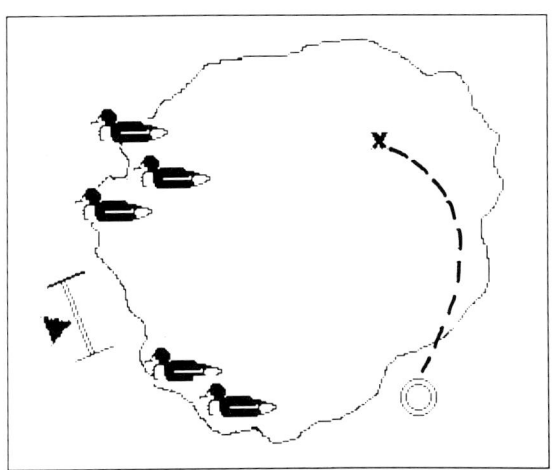

9. Watch out for bank running.

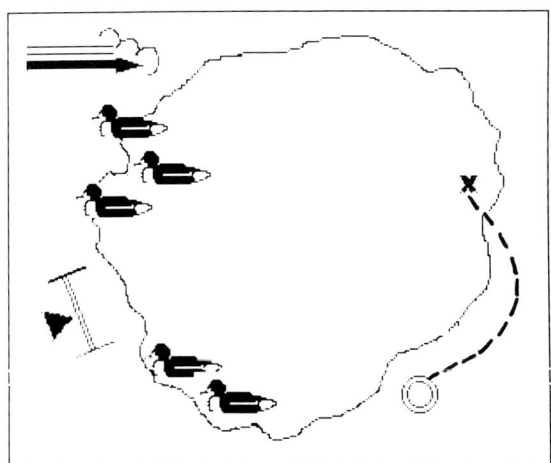

10. The dog has to get out of the water for the bird, then come back through the water.

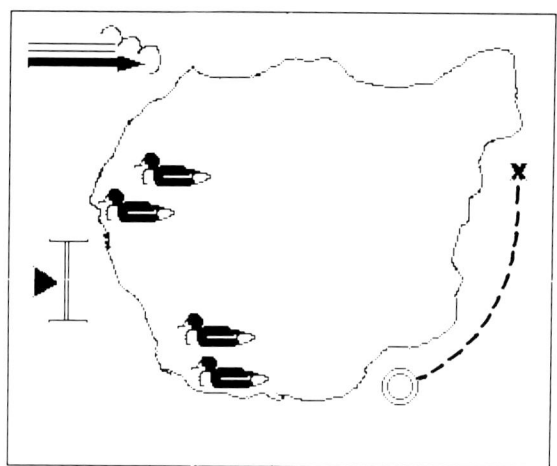

11. Move the line back---decoys are in the water.

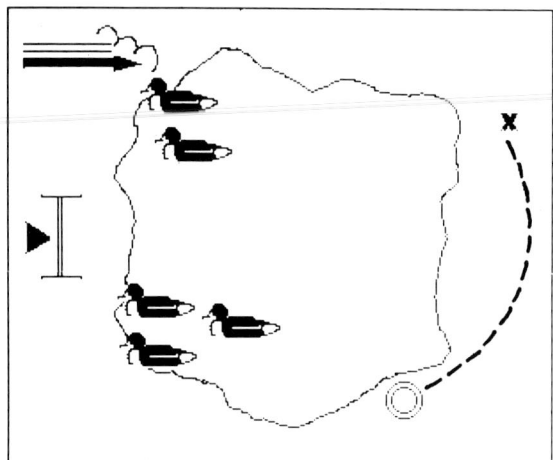

12.. Decoys act as a diversion.

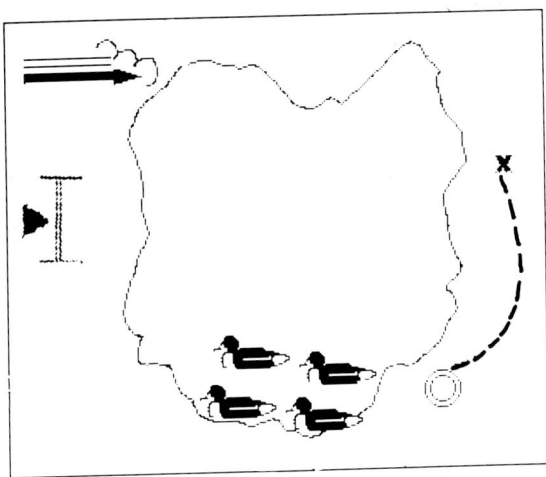

13. Dog has to swim past a point of land.

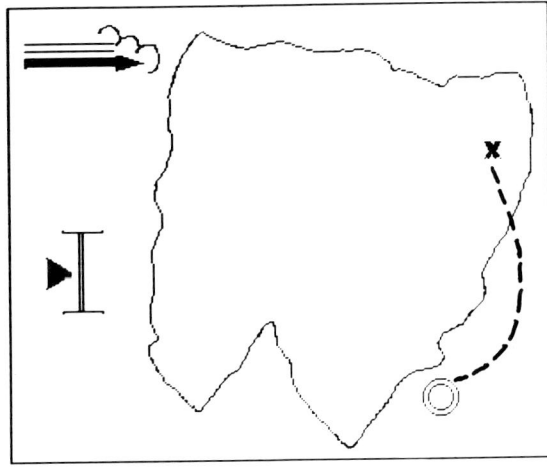

RETRIEVE *Medcalf*

14. Dog has to cross two bodies of water. The decoys will help draw the dog across.

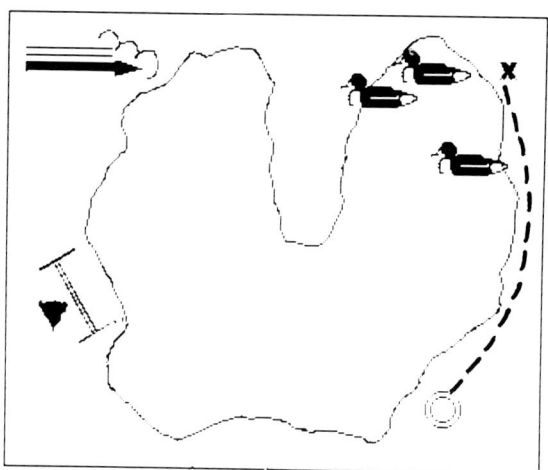

15. Move the decoys--makes this test more difficult.

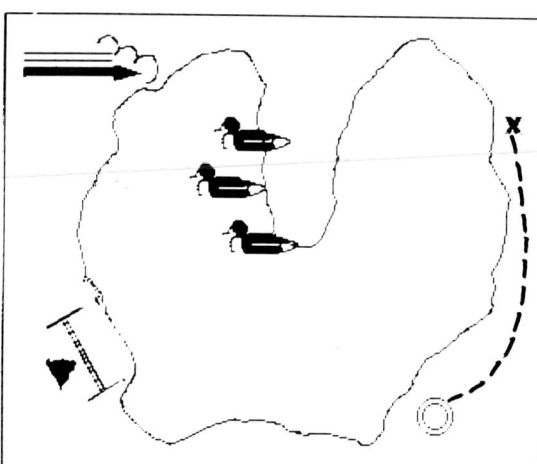

RETRIEVE   *SAMPLE TRAINING TESTS*

DOUBLES

1. Set up the test with a wide angle.
2. Run the dog on the memory bird as a single.
3. Run him on the double.
4. As the dog progresses, move the "line" farther back to tighten up the test, or move left or right.

Here are some samples.....

Land Doubles

1. No chance to switch here. Birds are thrown outside.

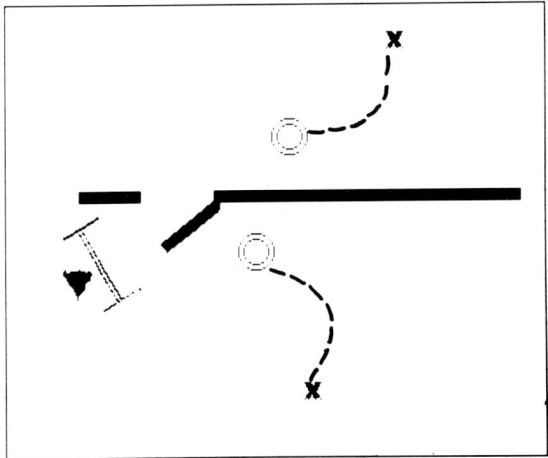

2. Move the line back-birds are thrown inside.

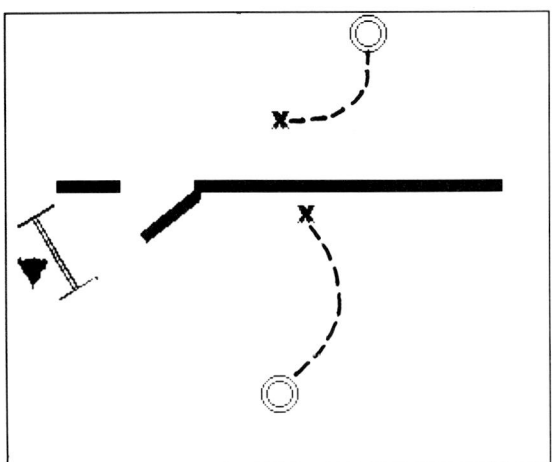

3. No fence---Keep a wide angle at first.

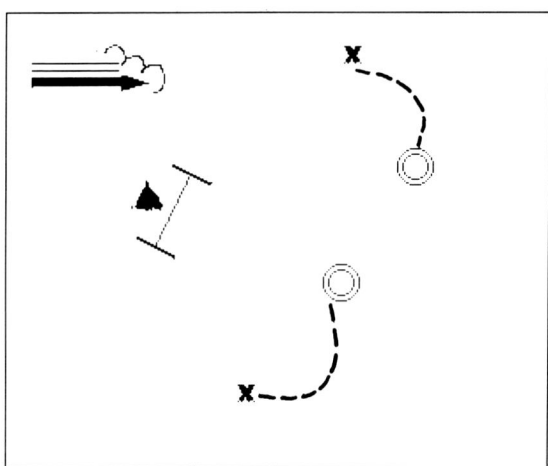

4. Moving the line decreases the angle and changes the distance to the birds.

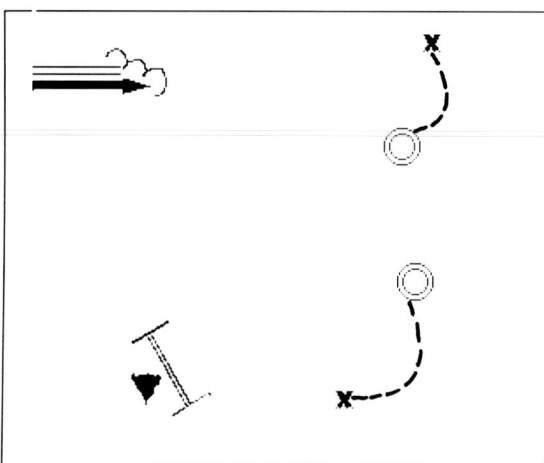

RETRIEVE   SAMPLE TRAINING TESTS

5. The wind makes this test more difficult. Scent from the short bird will draw the young dog back to the area.

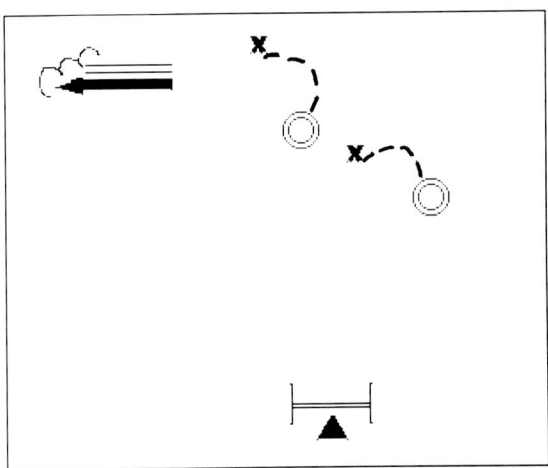

6. This should be easy.

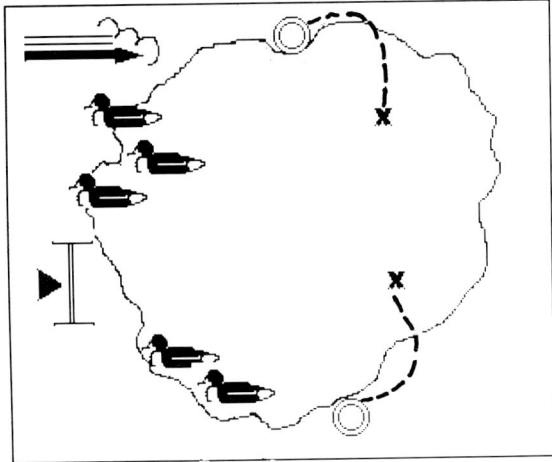

RETRIEVE   Medcalf

7. Change the line---makes it harder.

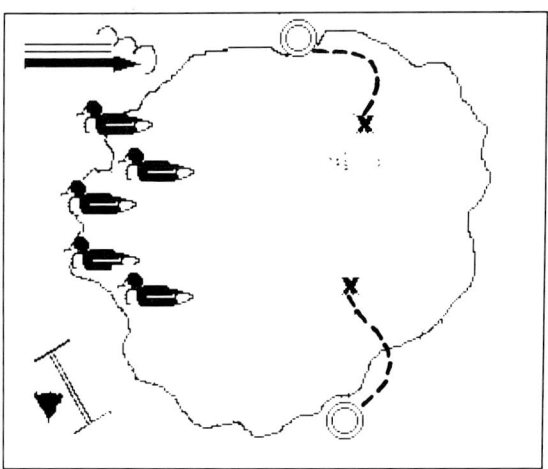

8. One wet---one dry.

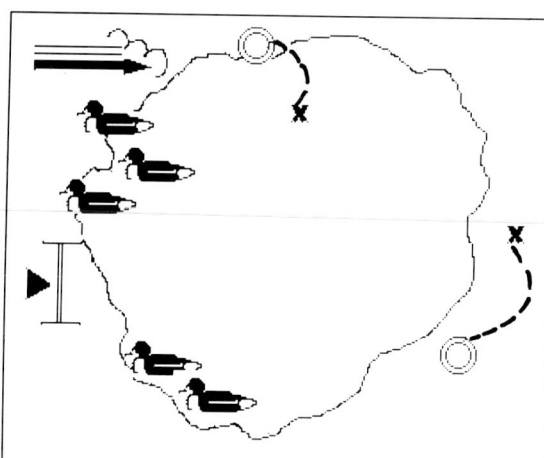

RETRIEVE   SAMPLE TRAINING TESTS

9. Do not set up a test that will teach bank running.

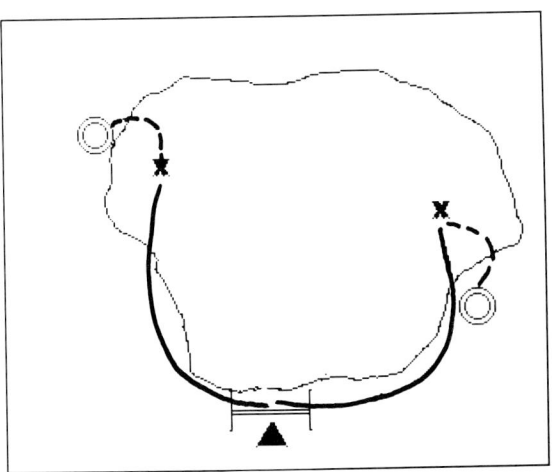

10. Easy triple.

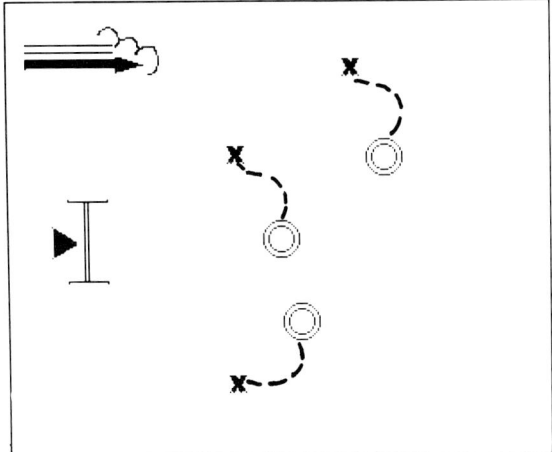

11. Move line to the side to make this test very difficult.

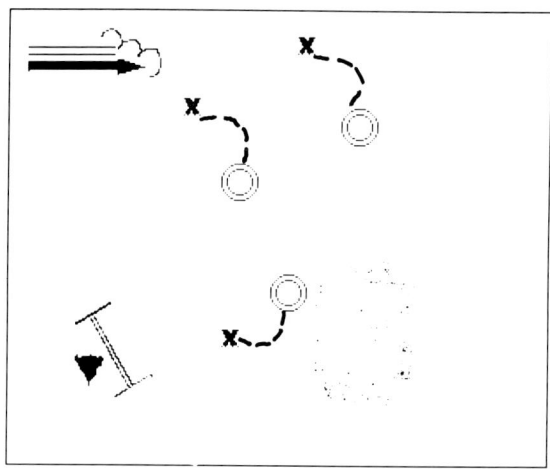

12. The last bird thrown short...makes this test easier.

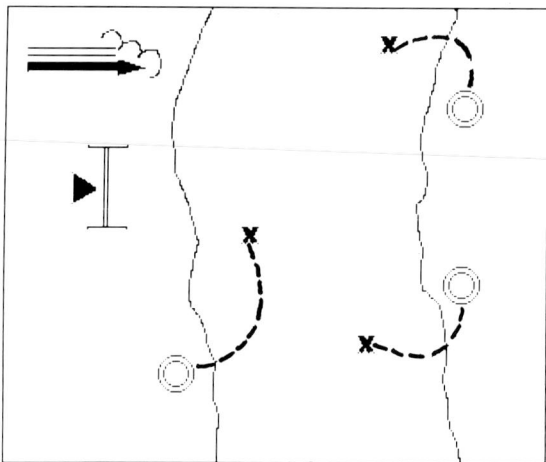

RETRIEVE SAMPLE TRAINING TESTS

13. Two in water-one on land. Move the land bird farther away from the water to increase difficulty.

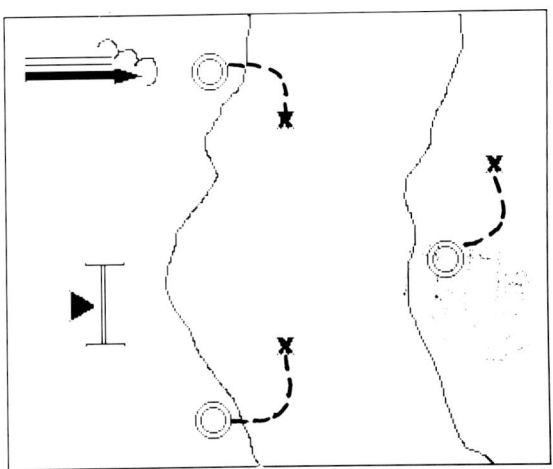

14. Triple down the bank...Very difficult.

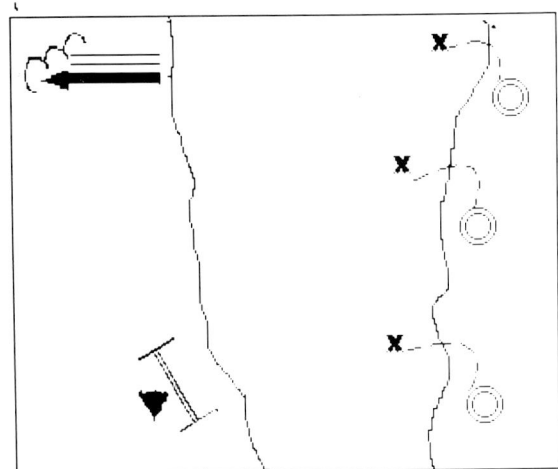

15. Plant all blinds downwind of the line.

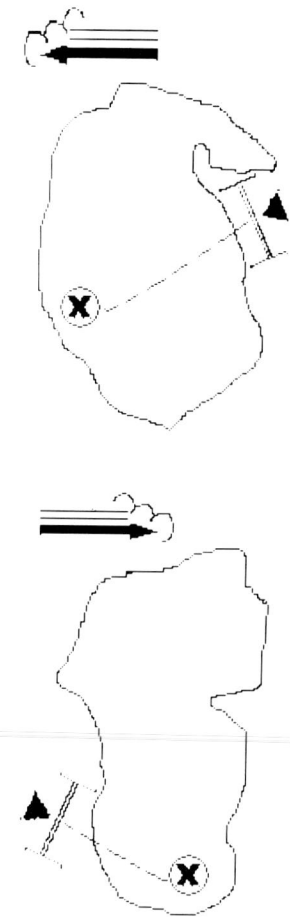

RETRIEVE   SAMPLE TRAINING TESTS

16. These will be much harder...The dog will be drawn toward the points.

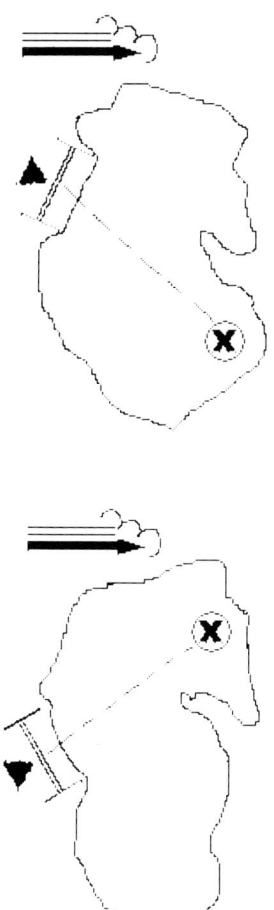

17. Double with a blind.

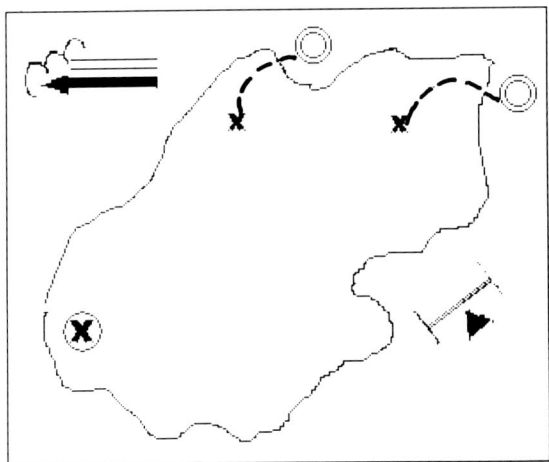

18. Double with blind planted between the two marks.

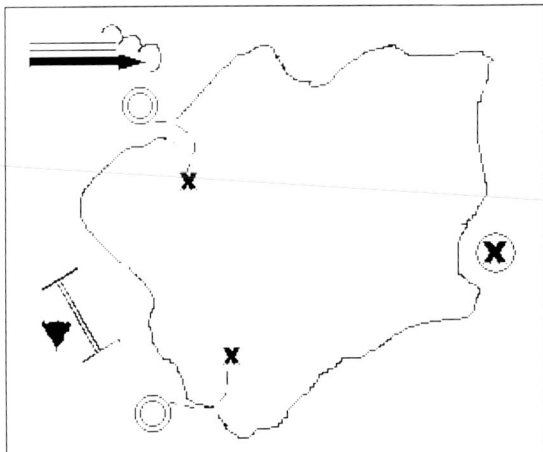

RETRIEVE   SAMPLE TRAINING TESTS

This is a typical tracking test. Drag a bird tied to a long pole. Walk on the downwind side of the track. Mark the track with flags so you can tell if the dog is on track.

```
                    <----------------50--75---------------->
                            X
                          X X X . . . . . . . . . . . . . . . . . . . . . .
                            X                                             :
    Scented area                                                          :
                                                                          :
       Wind------->                                                       :
                                                                          :
                                                              X    Bird
```

GLOSSARY OF TERMS

Back: The command you give a dog to tell him to retrieve.

Back: The command used to send a dog farther back after you have stopped him with a whistle.

Baseball Diamond: An imaginary ball field that is used to start teaching a dog to "handle."

Birdboy: Anyone who throws dummies, or birds. Also called gun, or gunners.

Blinker: A dog that knows where a bird is, but acts like he doesn't see it.

Book Matches: Paper matches that you pick up when you leave a restaurant. Used for "match stick enema," as opposed to a wooden, or "stick match."

Breaking: When a dog leaves the line, or starting point, before he is released with the command "back."

Breaking Strap: A piece of sash cord that is put around the dog's neck to keep him from breaking. (Leaving before sent)

Chest High Waders: Hip boots that are chest high.

Chessie: Chesapeake Bay Retriever

Choke Chain: A collar that is used for dog training.

Creep: When a dog does not stay at heel, but eases out in front of you before being sent to retrieve.

Cross: Same as the double cross. It has only one cross bar. Like a religious cross.

Decoy: An imitation of a duck that floats in the water to attract ducks.

Dysplasia: Abnormality of the hip joint.

Double: When two birds, or dummies are thrown for a dog to retrieve.

Double Cross: An imaginary cross, one hundred and fifty yards or more long, (resembles the cross on a Christmas Seal) that is used for teaching a dog to "handle" at longer distances than the "baseball diamond."

Dummy: An object that is thrown for the dog to retrieve.

Fall: When something is thrown for the dog to retrieve, the dog is to watch where it lands, or "mark the fall."

Fetch It Up: Get out there and pick up that bird!

Flier: A bird that is thrown and shot while it is flying.

Flush: To cause a bird, or birds to take to flight.

RETRIEVE   Medcalf

Foot Long Horseshoe: A piece of 3/8 or 1/2 inch metal rod that is bent into a horseshoe shape. It is driven into the ground and used as a stake, and training aid.

Golden Retriever: Considered by many to be the glamor dog of the retrieving breeds.

Gunshy: A dog that is afraid of noise is said to be gunshy.

Handling: To give a dog directions to a bird or dummy by use of whistle and hand signals.

Hardmouth: A dog that chews a bird badly enough to make it unfit for the table is said to be hardmouth.

Heavy Cover: Thick grass, or weeds. The dog can't see a dummy from more than a foot or so away in "heavy cover."

Heel: To sit, or walk at the side of the handler.

Here!: The command for the dog to come to you.

Honor: In some field trials a dog is required to sit, off leash, and watch another dog retrieve. That is called "honoring."

House Breaking: To teach a dog not to wet on the floor, or chew on things when he is in the house.

Lanyard: A cord that goes around your neck that is used to hold your whistle, and ear plugs.

Leash: A leather strap that snaps on a dog's collar. It is used to lead a dog.

RETRIEVE — GLOSSARY OF TERMS

Light Cover: Short grass. The dog can see a dummy from a long way off in light cover.

Line: There is a starting line. That is where your dog will sit while the birdboys are throwing the birds.

Line: You give the dog a "line", or direction to go when you are sending him after a hidden bird, or "blind."

Mark: When one or more birds are thrown for the dog, they are called marks. The dog has to "mark" the fall.

Over: The command for a dog to go left, or right when being handled to a blind.

Potty: To relieve himself. Urinate or defecate.

Piddle: Same as potty.

Poop: Same as piddle, or potty.

Quarter: When a dog runs back and forth in front of you in an attempt to flush birds.

Retriever-R-Trainer: A training aid that fires a retrieving dummy using a 22 cal. blank for propulsion.

Single: When only one bird is thrown for a dog.

Spraddle Legged: To sit on the ground, or floor with your legs spread out.

Swivel: A snap swivel goes on the end of a leash, and attaches to the dog's collar.

Take A Break: A command that releases the dog to that he can go potty, or piddle.

The Cross: Same as the double cross. It has only one cross bar. Like a religious cross.

Tracking: To follow a trail.

Triple: When three birds are thrown, or shot for a dog.

Yard Breaking: Teaching a dog to sit, stay, come, and heel.

Yellow Lab: A yellow, or beige colored Labrador Retriever.

QUICK REFERENCE FOR PROBLEMS

Chapter 3 DESIRE

1. Pup does not want to chase the sock. .... Pg. 15

2. Dog picks up sock, but will not bring it back. .... Pg. 16

3. Pup drops sock when I tug on leash. .... Pg. 16

Chapter 4 HOUSE BREAKING

1. What should I do when my dog has an "accident" on the floor. .... Pg. 24

2. My dog chews on furniture, shoes, and lamp cords. ..... Pg. 25

Chapter 5 YARD BREAKING

1. The choke chain doesn't slack off when I release pressure from the leash. .... Pg. 35

2. When my dog sits, he sits facing me, or some way other than at my side. .... Pg. 36

3. I tell my dog to "stay." When I walk away he slinks on his belly and tries to follow. .... Pg. 36

4. My dog runs away when I tell him to come. .... Pg. 38

Chapter 6 BIRDS AND SINGLES

1. When switching from socks to dummies, or from dummies to birds, the dog doesn't pick up the dummy. ...Pg. 51

2. Dog hunts short of the area of the fall. ....Pg. 51

Chapter 7 INTRODUCTION TO WATER

1. After several days of wading out in a pond, I still can't coax my dog into the water. ....Pg. 70

2. When my dog gets into the water, he swims around and plays, and refuses to come to me. ....Pg. 70

Chapter 8 STRAIGHT LINE TO THE BIRD

1. Running the bank. ....Pg. 74

2. My dog runs around heavy cover or obstacles no matter how many times I walk him through it. ....Pg. 75

Chapter 9 BY LAND AND SEA

1. My dog goes across the first water, but will not go any farther. ....Pg. 81

2. My dog will go across and pick up the bird, then he runs farther away, and will not come to me. ....Pg. 81

Chapter 11 WORKING OUT OF A BOAT

1. My dog will not jump out of a boat into deep water

RETRIEVE   QUICK REFERENCE FOR PROBLEMS

to retrieve. .... Pg. 88

2. The dog goes out of the boat O.K., but when he gets the dummy, he heads for the bank. .... Pg. 88

Chapter 12   DOUBLES ANYONE?

1. Switching. .... Pg. 94

2. After a long hunt without finding the bird, the dog leaves the area. .... Pg. 95

3. The dog retrieves the first bird O.K., but refuses to go for the second one. .... Pg. 96

4. The dog brings the first bird back, drops it close by, and then takes off for the other one. .... Pg. 97

5. My dog is so anxious to retrieve that he creeps several feet in front of me when the bird is thrown. .... Pg. 97

Chapter 13   TAKING A LINE

1. The dog picks up the first dummy, but on the next retrieve he goes back to where the first one was and stops. .... Pg. 101

2. The dog refuses to go. Acts as if he does not know what I want. .... Pg. 102

3. The dog runs to the first dummy in the line, and then leaves to pick up the second. .... Pg. 103

Chapter 14 LINING IN WATER

1. When sport is returning with a dummy through weeds, the clothespin tangles and jerks the dummy from him. .... Pg. 106

Chapter 15 HANDLING

1. The baseball diamond... Pg. 111

2. Can't learn hand signals. .... Pg. 124

3. The dog will take a line out about twenty yards, stop, and wait for another command. .... Pg. 124

4. Near sighted. The dog will not go beyond 75 yards .... Pg. 125

5. Hard of hearing. The dog will go on a straight line for 100 yards or so, and then start to wander. Apparently cannot hear the whistle. .... Pg. 127

6. The dog goes out of sight when sent on a "blind". .... Pg. 128

Chapter 16 QUARTER AND FLUSH

1. Dog is distracted by noise from the gun. .... Pg. 139

2. Dog "breaks" on fliers. .... Pg. 139

Index

ACCIDENT 24

BACK 114, 119

BANK RUNNING 74
BASEBALL 112
BIRDBOYS 45
BIRDS 43
BLIND 99, 149
BLINDS 72
BLINKING 44
BOAT (RETRIEVING FROM) 87, 89
BREAKING 48, 139
BREAKING STRAP 47, 48, 97

CHEATING 72
CHEWING 23, 25
CHOKE CHAIN 33, 35
COME HERE 31
CREEPING 97
CROSS PATTERN 122

DECOYS 83
DIVERSION 91
DOUBLES 91, 145
DYSPLASIA 12

EQUIPMENT LIST	5
FOOT LONG HORSESHOE	37, 111
FORCE TO HOLD	17
GLOSSARY OF TERMS	180, 182, 184
GUNSHY	34
HANDLING	111, 122, 147, 149, 151
HARD OF HEARING	127
HARDMOUTH	44, 45
HEEL	33, 34
HOUSE BREAKING	19, 21, 23, 25, 27
JUMPING UP	32
LIE DOWN	31
LINE	99, 105, 127, 148
MARK	91
MATCH STICK ENEMA	21, 22
MEMORY BIRD	91, 96
NEAR SIGHTED	125
OVER	112, 114
PICK UP YOUR DOG	128
PICKING A PUP	11
POPPING	115
PROBLEMS (QUICK REFERENCE)	185, 187

QUARTER AND FLUSH	137
REFUSALS	96
RETRIEVE-R-TRAINER	125
RUNNING AWAY	38
SIT	29, 30
STAKE	37
STAY	29, 30, 36
STOP AT FLUSH	137
SWITCH	94
TRACKING	141
TRAINING TEST	157--179
TRAINING TIPS	144, 146
TRIPLE	92
WAGON WHEEL	101
WATER	65, 67, 69
WHISTLE	73, 100, 112
WHISTLE SIGNALS	147
YARD BREAKING	29